EMPLOYEE
ENGAGEMENT
FUNDAMENTALS

A guide for
managers &
supervisors

Marc Drizin
Stephen P. Hundley, Ph.D.

WorldatWork.

About WorldatWork®

WorldatWork (www.worldatwork.org) is a global human resources association focused on compensation, benefits, work-life and integrated total rewards to attract, motivate and retain a talented workforce. Founded in 1955, WorldatWork provides a network of more than 30,000 members and professionals in 75 countries with training, certification, research, conferences and community. It has offices in Scottsdale, Arizona, and Washington, D.C.

©2008 WorldatWork Press

ISBN 978-1-57963-194-9

Editor: Andrea Ozias

Cover Design: Melissa Neubauer

Production Manager: Rebecca Williams Ficker

WorldatWork.
The Total Rewards Association

www.worldatwork.org

TABLE OF CONTENTS

PREFACE

"Employees quit a boss, not a company." This phrase may seem both overly simple and a bit harsh. However, the bluntness of this statement should not distract from its significance. Finding, keeping and motivating employees represent some of the biggest management challenges facing today's organizations. Successful managers realize their employees are, in fact, one of the most important resources in creating a sustainable competitive advantage in the marketplace.

Employee knowledge generates new products, services and solutions. Employee behaviors can facilitate improved customer service and lead to customer loyalty. And employee attitudes can enhance the overall work experience for others in the organization, including the desire to work hard, help colleagues and maintain positive working relationships. Thus, employees can — and do — contribute to the organization's ability to succeed and competitively differentiate itself from rival firms.

An employee's willingness (and even desire) to work hard, stay longer, behave ethically and get along with co-workers is, among other things, largely dependent on the extent to which the individual employee enjoys positives relationships in the workplace. *The most important relationship an employee has in the workplace is with his/her manager or supervisor.* In recent years, and with the widespread use of teams through which interdependent work must be performed, the notion of important relationships in the workplace has extended to include colleagues and co-workers, in addition to the employee's manager. Thus, the nature of these relationships informs employee attitudes, intentions and behaviors. In turn, these determine the degree of loyalty and engagement an individual puts forth in the pursuit of both individual and organizational objectives.

This book is designed to assist managers and supervisors with strategies and approaches to engaging their employees. Indeed, this book is both a follow-up to and companion piece of the authors' 2007 book, *Workforce Engagement: Strategies to Attract, Motivate and Retain Talent.* In that book, a more comprehensive, organization-wide agenda for workforce engagement is presented, and it includes data, concepts and case studies. This book, meanwhile, is more focused on manager and supervisor roles related to the topic.

Many worthwhile approaches to managing and supervising employees focus on issues related to gender, race/ethnicity, generational gaps and other personally identifiable characteristics of employees. This book takes a slightly different approach: Employees are identified and described based on their likely position in what the authors term "the employment life cycle." How a new employee is managed and engaged differs, necessarily, from how a long-term employee is treated by the boss. Similarly, a recently transferred or promoted employee should be managed and engaged differently than a temporary employee. Thus, managers and supervisors should find that the 10 types of employees discussed in this book resonate with how they might view where many of their employees are situated in the employment life cycle.

Employee Engagement Fundamentals: A Guide for Managers & Supervisors organizes the various employee types around the employment life cycle, and presents each in individual chapters. One important note: There often are cases in which employees may fall into more than one employment life cycle category. For example, a *mid-career employee* also may be an *underperforming employee*, and this may be due to the fact that this is an *employee with special needs or circumstances* requiring managerial intervention. In attempting to provide useful information for readers in a fairly straightforward, accessible manner, the authors purposely avoid articulating all of the various combinations that might exist in today's pluralistic, diverse workplaces.

The book concludes by presenting useful information to assist in enhancing managerial effectiveness through employee engagement. This provides ways to identify outcomes of employee engagement, presents 10 principles every manager or supervisor should know, and provides a call to action to evaluate and improve management-related employee engagement practices inside the organization. While no one publication can provide complete and definitive advice for managers, this book should enhance managerial awareness of, interest in and action toward creating and sustaining organizations that find, keep and engage the best talent.

Employee Engagement Fundamentals: A Guide for Managers & Supervisors is published by WorldatWork, the total rewards association. In this context, total rewards refers to all of the tools available to the employer that may be used to attract, motivate and retain employees. Total rewards includes everything the employee perceives to be of value resulting from the employment relationship. This book provides a framework for understanding employee engagement as part of a broader total rewards strategy.

chapter 1
INTRODUCTION TO WORKFORCE ENGAGEMENT

What Is Workforce Engagement, and Why Is It Important?

Workforce engagement is defined as an ongoing process to recruit, retrain, reward and retain productive and effective employees by enhancing understanding of organizational practices and employee priorities, attitudes, behaviors and intentions.

What are the essential elements in this definition?

First, as an ongoing process, ideas associated with workforce engagement are continually evolving, with new ideas frequently introduced. Second, workforce engagement applies to every aspect of employment — recruiting, retraining, rewarding and retaining employees — and is not a one-time intervention. Third, workforce engagement takes into account not just individual employee performance, but attitudes, intentions and priorities as well.

Thus, the fundamental ideas of workforce engagement encompass both *philosophy and strategy*. That is, an organizational commitment to workforce engagement involves a set of beliefs about enhancing workforce performance, and particular activities to achieve them. Now that workforce engagement has been defined, and the relationship to the companion text explained, let's examine the "Four R's" of workforce engagement.

The 'Four R's' of Workforce Engagement

- **Recruit** — Find the right talent, for the right job, at the right time.
- **Retrain** — Equip employees with the knowledge and skills to continuously perform meaningful work.
- **Reward** — Recognize achievements through monetary, performance management and other means.
- **Retain** — Keep the right talent, in the right job, for the right amount of time.

Recruit

When organizations recruit employees, they seek to *find the right talent, for the right job, at the right time.* Inherent in this process is a sound understanding of the job, its specific requirements and the relationship the job has to the overall organization. Once that is defined, organizations can tap recruitment sources that likely will yield the best candidates. The continued and anticipated marketplace demands for the company's products or services are the main factor in determining the need for additional talent. Other considerations affecting an ability to effectively recruit talent include the level of competition in the market, the present composition of the organization's employee resources and the availability of skilled individuals in the labor markets in which the organization conducts business.

Retrain

After recruiting talent, organizations need to *equip employees with the knowledge, skills, perspective and experiences to continuously perform meaningful work.* Even when employees enter the organization with significant work experience or educational attainment, it is crucial that the company provide training on the organization's own way of doing business. Equally important, however, is the need to ensure that such training is ongoing, thus permitting employees to continuously learn the competencies needed to remain a viable, value-adding team member.

Reward

The ability to *recognize individual, team and organizational achievements by monetary and other performance management incentives* is the centerpiece to an effective employee reward system. While pay is important, numerous studies conclude that simply rewarding employees with cash is not sufficient to motivate them to achieve sustainable performance. Worse, however, is the unintended consequence of potentially "trapping" an employee who might want to leave the organization, but feels that he/she would be unable to earn as much elsewhere. Thus, rewarding employees should be a holistic endeavor in which cash compensation is one of several major components that also include benefits, access to training, development and other professional opportunities, organizational perks and positive feedback.

Retain

One measure of workforce stability is an organization's turnover rate, or the percentage of employees retained by the company during a given time frame.

Keeping the right talent, in the right job, for the right amount of time is necessary if the organization is to realize success in designing products and services, deepening relationships with customers and business partners, and growing the base of intellectual capital within the company. There are both real and hidden costs associated with employee turnover. Real costs include the actual financial consequence of losing talent, in having to recruit and retrain a new employee, and in lost productivity and revenue that result when an unanticipated vacancy occurs. Hidden costs include the lower morale that could emerge given the instability of the organization's employees, the potential for poor or inconsistent service to customers, and the loss of intellectual capital that is hard to replace. Although employee retention should be a key organizational goal, it is important to view retention in the context of occupational or industry trends or norms.

Organizational Practices Contributing to Workforce Engagement

- **Strategic Issues** — effective senior leadership; reputation management; ethics, diversity and safety; and stakeholder input
- **Core HR Processes** — workforce selection; organizational orientation; training and development; rewards and recognition; and work-life balance
- **Operational Components** — performance management; tools and technology; opportunities for advancement; and daily satisfaction

Workforce engagement encompasses organizational practices that permeate all levels of the organization, from senior leaders to individual-contributor employees. Thirteen components of workforce engagement have been identified and are grouped under three broad umbrellas: strategic issues, core HR processes and operational components.

Strategic Issues
Strategic issues are top-level, organizationwide approaches that support workforce engagement. These include:

- *Effective Senior Leadership* — the ability of organizational leaders to articulate a meaningful strategy; recognize the relationship between workforce engagement and organizational success; model effective leadership behaviors; and create a high-performance culture.
- *Reputation Management* — the ability of organizational leaders to shape and manage the organization's reputation internally and externally; identify and

describe strengths of the organization's products, services and solutions; and exercise positive corporate social responsibility.

- *Ethics, Diversity and Safety* — the ability of organizational leaders to create a culture of ethical conduct and decision-making; comply with laws and policies; respect and manage diversity; and ensure a safe work environment.
- *Stakeholder Input* — the ability of organizational leaders to seek regular feedback from customers, business partners and others; benchmark with other organizations on effective practices; measure employee perceptions; and improve work and other organizational experiences.

Core HR Processes

Core HR processes are activities that help acquire, orient, develop and reward an engaged workforce. These include:

- *Workforce Selection* — the ability of HR professionals to assist the organization by designing meaningful job and work experiences; outlining hiring criteria and competencies; developing effective recruitment methods; and implementing appropriate selection processes.
- *Organizational Orientation* — the ability of HR professionals to assist the organization by developing processes for effective employee integration; educating employees about organizational values and business practices; and developing relevant orientation, mentoring and coaching programs.
- *Training and Development* — the ability of HR professionals to assist the organization by assessing needs and establishing priorities for training; designing appropriate performance improvement approaches; and implementing and evaluating training and development activities.
- *Rewards and Recognition* — the ability of HR professionals to assist the organization by rewarding performance through a variety of approaches; recognizing employee contributions to organizational achievements; ensuring fair treatment in reward practices; and developing strategies for employee involvement.
- *Work-Life Balance* — the ability of HR professionals to assist the organization by creating approaches for employees to effectively balance personal,
work and community responsibilities; developing flexible approaches to work, as feasible; and managing stress, promoting wellness and avoiding employee burnout.

Operational Components

Operational components are the managerial and supervisory responsibilities necessary for workforce engagement. These include:

- *Performance Management* — the ability of managers and supervisors to identify relevant dimensions of employee performance; set challenging and meaningful expectations; monitor and evaluate performance; and provide regular and constructive feedback to employees.

- *Tools and Technology* — the ability of managers and supervisors to allocate resources necessary for employee work; provide tools and techniques for job performance; ensure ergonomically correct work environments; and appropriately structure work flow, interactions and processes.

- *Opportunities for Advancement* — the ability of managers and supervisors to promote from within or provide lateral mobility to employees; identify, develop and, in some cases, release marginal, difficult or improper-fit employees; and effectively handle downsizing, outsourcing or discontinuation of work.

- *Daily Satisfaction* — the ability of managers and supervisors to recognize what motivates employees to come to work each day; ensure working relationships are positive; allow for autonomy and discretion in job performance; show respect to employees; and maintain a high-performance, enjoyable workplace.

Employee Perspectives That Contribute to Workforce Engagement

- Priorities
- Attitudes
- Behaviors
- Intentions

Organizational practices represent one side of the workforce engagement scale, while employee perspectives from the other side. Indeed, individual employees each hold specific priorities, attitudes, behaviors and intentions about their work. These perspectives help influence the extent to which an employee is retained by and engaged in the organization, or whether he/she will seek to leave.

Priorities

Employee priorities are defined as the degree to which an individual seeks participation in the workforce; values participation in the workforce; and views work as a primary activity. Priorities are informed, in part, by personal, circumstantial and environmental considerations.

For example, a new mother may seek to remain at home with her child rather than return to work, thus redefining her priorities related to work. Intrinsic motivation, or the personal enjoyment or fulfillment one receives from performing a job, also informs an employee's workplace priority. Additionally, extrinsic pressures (e.g., debt and other financial issues) may compel participation in the workforce.

Attitudes

Employee attitudes are defined as the extent to which an individual:

- Feels positively or negatively about the organization, his/her job and workplace relationships
- Enjoys or dislikes coming to work on a daily basis
- Views organizational practices as being relatively consistent with his/her personal values, beliefs and expectations.

These attitudes are informed, in part, by specific organizational policies, business processes and people with whom an individual must interact. Individual perceptions about the organization's treatment of its employees, compared to the perceptions of how other organizations treat employees, also affect employee attitudes. Finally, the nature of work performed by the individual can contribute to a positive or negative attitude.

Behaviors

Employee behaviors are defined as the specific ways in which an individual:

- Performs work consistent with job requirements, organizational needs and industry standards
- Seeks to work effectively with various stakeholders (e.g., co-workers, supervisors, customers, suppliers and business partners)
- Adheres to the organization's expectations, policies and practices.

Behaviors are informed, in part, by a sound fit between the individual and his/her organization, job and responsibilities; explicitly defined expectations for performance processes and outcomes; ongoing, constructive feedback; and access to appropriate training and development opportunities.

Intentions

Finally, employee intentions are defined as the likelihood that an individual:

- Remains with or leaves the organization in the foreseeable future

- Seeks advancement opportunities either within the organization or from elsewhere
- Continues exhibiting behaviors necessary for effective job performance.

Such intentions are informed, in part, by the priorities an individual holds about work in general, and the job and organization in particular; the attributes an individual holds toward the organization, the job and his/her workplace relationships; and the behaviors an individual exhibits through his/her job performance.

What We Know About the Nature of Workforce Engagement

Much of the thought behind workforce engagement initially is based on a background of customer satisfaction and loyalty. When employees are engaged, they are much more likely to behave in ways that benefit customer loyalty, retention and business success. Meyer and Allen, in their book *Commitment in the Workplace*, put forth three types of employee commitment:

- Normative commitment, when employees feel obligated to stay
- Continuance commitment, when employees feel trapped and as if they have to stay with the organization
- Affective commitment, when employees stay because they want to.

It is this affective commitment, or the feeling of personal and psychological attachment to an organization, that creates the employee attitudes necessary for workforce engagement. However, attitudes by themselves are not enough. Employees also need to behave in ways that benefit the organization, and it is the combination of behaviors and attitudes that help create workforce engagement. (See "Behaviors and Actions Necessary for Business Success.")

Three workforce engagement national benchmark studies, all using a Web-based panel populated with both consumer and business demographics, were conducted by Employee Hold'em in 2004-05, 2006-07 and 2008-09. In the "2004-05 National Workforce Engagement Benchmark Study," 2,553 employees were included; 1,826 were included for the 2006-07 study; and 2,368 employees in the most recent (at press time) 2008-09 study. The final data is weighted to match the U.S. Bureau of Labor Statistics on gender, age, industry and geography, and each national benchmark has had an R^2 ranging from 0.65 to 0.70.

To inform the national benchmark studies, research was conducted on best practices used by a host of HR consultancies and practitioners, such as Hay Group, Watson Wyatt Worldwide, Walker Information, Gallup and Hewitt Associates. In addition, leading industry associations and organizations, such as the Society for Human Resource Management, HR.com, WorldatWork, the American Society for

Behaviors and Actions Necessary for Business Success

- Recommending the organization as a good place to work
- Staying with the company for the next two years
- Doubting negative press heard about the company
- Being highly motivated to work hard
- Going the extra mile for customers
- Working hard as a team member
- Participating in training and development opportunities
- Advocating for the company even after employment ends.

Training and Development and the American Management Association, provided insight through national and international studies conducted with companies around the world. In addition, decades of experience with hundreds of HR consultants and clients and hundreds of thousands of employees worldwide provided a unique perspective on the building of the Employee Hold'em workforce engagement benchmark.

Although the benchmark studies used as the basis for this book may seem similar to other retention models, these measure engagement, the combination of commitment and behavior, and the specific work factors that affect engagement. The national benchmark studies marry the strategic and the tactical, the scientific and the common sense. Thus, this model of engagement also includes a competitive assessment of eight individual factors affecting employee retention that are unique among other models of engagement. In an era in which employees have choice, this is a critical element to measure.

The Levels of Workforce Engagement

Workforce engagement is a combination of both the attitudes of employees and their likelihood to exhibit the types of behaviors that make companies successful, specifically their likelihood to stay, go the extra mile for customers and recommend the organization as a great place to work. To better understand the dynamics of engagement inside an organization, employees are divided into three engagement groups:

- *Fully Engaged* — These employees have a strong personal or psychological attachment to their organization, and will act in ways that benefit their customers and their organization. These employees are the most likely to stay longer, work harder and recommend the company as a good place to work. They are the stars who will not only meet customer requirements, but will exceed them on a consistent basis. However, don't assume that employee tenure necessarily equates to engagement. Numerous research studies have shown that just because employees stay with a company, it doesn't necessarily mean they are behaving in ways that continue to help the company be successful.

- *Reluctant* — These employees may act in ways that benefit the company. Some employees may have other priorities that affect their ability to fully commit to their organization, such as new moms who want to stay home with their children, spouses who are leaving town and taking their spouse (the employee) with them, or a team member who just wants to change careers. These types of situations normally account for a small percentage of reluctant team members.

  Far more serious are those reluctant workers who do not have a strong commitment to the organization, and therefore are much less likely to go the extra mile for customers. These are the employees who are reluctant to leave and reluctant to work hard. They may be scared to find other employment because they feel as if they don't have the skills necessary to find another job, or other jobs may not be available.

  Most worrisome are those employees trapped with golden handcuffs that keep them retained because they have to be, not because they want to be. Although a company will retain these employees either way, this subtle difference makes all the difference in the world to clients and the level of support they receive from employees.

- *Unengaged* — These employees may be the least desirable of all the workforce engagement groups. They do not have a positive relationship with the company, and have sent their résumés out to competitors. In some cases, they may try to harm existing relationships with customers or suppliers, or may try to steal company secrets. Even if they have one foot out the door, one foot still resides in the company, making the management of this portion of the workforce vital.

Highlights from the National Workforce Engagement Benchmark Studies

With more jobs than there are employees to fill them, companies need to be ever more vigilant on the impact supervisors and managers have on workforce engagement and employee retention. In the 2004-05, 2006-07 and 2008-09 national workforce engagement benchmark studies, the importance of the supervisor-employee relationship is apparent. Consider:

- When employees believe their supervisors perform well, 7-in-10 are *fully engaged* — ready to go the extra mile for customers and help out other members of the team. When they don't see their supervisors as a positive force, only 1-in-4 are *fully engaged*.
- Employees who did not feel positively about their supervisors in 2004-05 and 2006-07 were five times more likely to be *unengaged* than employees who did (49 percent versus 10 percent). The difference is even more pronounced in 2008-09: while 46 percent of employees who do not have a good impression about their supervisor are *unengaged*, just 3 percent of employees with a positive impression of their relationship with their supervisor are *unengaged*.
- Nine-in-ten employees with a positive impression of their supervisors are affectively committed to their organization. These are employees who "feel like part of the family," consider "company problems to be their own problems, too," have a "strong personal or psychological attachment to the company," and "feel strongly committed to making the company successful." When employees had a neutral or negative impression of their supervisors, 8 percent had the same level of commitment to their organization.

In addition:
- In 2004-05 and 2006-07, employees with a negative attitude toward their supervisor were four times more likely to be "not very" or "not at all" motivated to work hard compared to employees with positive attitudes (11 percent versus 3 percent). In 2008-09, less than 1 percent of employees with a positive attitude toward their supervisor were not motivated to work hard.
- Employees with a negative attitude toward their supervisor were more than four times more likely to be "not very" or "not at all" likely to provide enthusiastic referrals for their company (23 percent versus 5 percent) in 2004-05 and 2006-07. In 2008-09, less than 1 percent of employees with a positive attitude would refrain from providing enthusiastic referrals.
- Employees with a positive attitude toward their supervisor are more than twice as likely to be "extremely" or "very" likely to remain with the company even if offered a similar job with slightly higher pay (75 percent versus 37 percent in 2008-09).

In both 2006-07 and 2008-09, only three-quarters (77 percent) of all employees agreed they had "a good relationship with their immediate supervisor," a significant decrease from 2004-05 levels of 80 percent. In 2008-09:

- Less than 8-in-10 employees (77 percent) working in companies with 100-249 people felt positively about their supervisor relationship, while significantly fewer (65 percent) employees in companies with 5,000 to 10,000 employees felt the same. In fact, nearly 1-in-8 employees of the largest companies (5,000 to 10,000 employees and 10,000 or more employees) disagreed they had a good relationship with their boss (12 percent).
- Executives and senior management were the most positive in their feelings about their immediate supervisor (90 percent positive), while there was no statistical difference in the feelings of supervisors or individual contributors (those employees who do not supervise others).
- Supervisors who encourage their employees to participate in company-sponsored social events and provide employees with work-related training and education are viewed significantly more positively than supervisors who didn't support these same initiatives.
- Employees living in the South (South Atlantic, East South Central and West South Central census regions) were the most positive, with nearly 8-in-10 employees (79 percent) agreeing they have a good relationship with their immediate supervisor, while more than 2-in-3 New England and East North Central census region employees (68 percent) felt the same.

A "Supervisory Index" is made up of questions from various work factors in the Employee Hold'em model of workforce engagement and retention. These work factors include:

- Daily satisfaction
- Opportunities for advancement
- Organizational orientation
- Rewards and recognition
- Training and development
- Performance management
- Tools and technology
- Work-life balance.

Further details on these questions will be explored in the coming chapters. Additionally, readers may visit the Employee Hold'em Web site (www.employeeholdem.com) for more information on study methodology, results, implications and other resources.

The Various Employee Types That Managers Must Engage

- New employees
- Mid-career employees
- Underperforming employees
- Superstar employees
- Returning employees
- Transferred or promoted employees
- Long-term employees
- Temporary employees
- Distance-based employees
- Employees with special needs or circumstances

New Employees

New employees represent individuals who are literally the "new kids on the block" and have no prior employment history with the organization. They tend to bring fresh perspectives and new ideas to the workplace. When initially hired, they are excited, tend to view the organization through rose-colored glasses and actually believe what they are told.

Mid-Career Employees

These employees have been with the organization three to five years. They tend to be the "worker bees" and blend into their work surroundings. They may not get managerial attention (new and bad employees tend to get this), and the excitement of the job may have worn off. These same employees are headhunter ready and may be looking to either advance or leave the organization.

Underperforming Employees

These are individuals who, for whatever reason, are not meeting expectations. They may be reluctant and/or unengaged employees, individuals with an "improper" fit to the job or organization, or just plain old bad apples. They still are expected to do minimally acceptable work and, because they interact with customers and colleagues, these employees can jeopardize stakeholder relationships.

Superstar Employees

Superstar employees tend to be top-grade talent and may, in fact, represent the 20 percent of employees who do 80 percent of the work. These high-achieving employees always are counted on to exceed customer expectations, will take on new initiatives and can model desired behavior to others. While these employees may be potential leaders inside the organization, they also are the most desirable for rival firms to steal.

Returning Employees

This employee type represents individuals who left the organization and now are rejoining the company. They may have left for personal, academic or professional reasons, or may be returning because the grass wasn't as green elsewhere. Regardless, these individuals typically hit the ground running, usually have little to no rehire costs and may have picked up new skills elsewhere. While rehiring former employees may be positive from a PR standpoint, it also can pose unique challenges and opportunities for managers.

Transferred or Promoted Employees

These individuals have had lateral or upward movement in the organization. They typically are technically proficient, are viewed as up-and-comers, and usually are responsible for meeting tactical goals. Because their impact on employees and customers is so great, these individuals may make or break workforce engagement strategies.

Long-Term Employees

These employees have been with the organization five years or longer. They are viewed as "friends and family" and provide tremendous intellectual and organizational capital. These employees possess deep knowledge, relationships and history with multiple stakeholders, may be the external face of the company and might be seen as de facto internal leaders. At the same time, some long-term employees pose tremendous challenges to managers in maintaining and enhancing their ongoing engagement at work.

Temporary Employees

These employees typically are hired to fill short-term "production" problems. They may be seasonal or contingent employees who, in many cases, have similar responsibilities as more traditional employees. Individuals who also are employees of another organization (e.g., a staffing agency) may possess a "duality of loyalty" that poses challenges. Finally, there also may be legal, practical and managerial limitations when independent contractors — who cannot be treated as employees — also perform work in the organization.

Distance-Based Employees

These employees perform either a portion or all of their job at locations different from their manager. These individuals are geographically dispersed, telecommuters, satellite-office workers and mobile workers, and they may be minimally, moderately or highly distant. There are unique organizational and managerial challenges in communicating with, monitoring and keeping these types of employees connected and engaged.

Employees with Special Needs or Circumstances

This group is the personification of workplace diversity. It comprises individuals who are physically and/or mentally challenged as well as employees who require managerial accommodations or interventions that have nothing to do with physical or mental limitations. Employees who have outside personal, academic, community and/or other obligations, while trying to balance professional responsibilities, fall into this category. Thus, one could argue that literally every single employee ultimately falls into this category.

chapter 2
ENGAGING NEW EMPLOYEES

Who Are *New Employees,* and Why Are They Important?

While seemingly obvious, new employees are those individuals who have no prior employment history with the organization. They represent a significant investment on the part of the organization because recruitment, selection, placement, orientation and training, among other things, all are direct costs the organization has undertaken to bring the new employee into the fold.

These new hires — whom we may instinctively refer to as "new kids on the block" — may, in fact, have more experience than many existing employees. Career mobility in the new economy now encourages (and sometimes forces) individuals to have multiple jobs with several different employers throughout their working years. Thus, someone might be "new" to the organization, yet be vastly experienced in his/her field, occupation or industry.

How "new" employees are — or the nature of how experienced employees are when they start a new job — may affect how they are initially managed. Highly skilled employees, such as nurses, may be treated differently than an entry-level manufacturing or retail worker because, presumably, the nurse has a level of educational attainment and professional credentialing that indicates proficiencies in a distinct career.

New employees bring fresh perspectives and new ideas to the organization. They are excited about their work and the prospect of joining a new organization; thus, new employees may tend to view the firm through rose-colored glasses and initially believe what they were told during the recruitment/selection/orientation process. Managers should recognize that it often is these new employees who may be "let down" by the subsequent actions of the organization — thus shattering or altering their initial view of the company and its employees. As such, new employees might lose their initial enthusiasm when they realize that managers' actions don't align with their espoused values — managers who do not "walk the talk."

From a business standpoint, managers have an obligation to treat new employees with care, and to ensure that employees feel positively and want to behave in ways that benefit the company — namely working hard, staying longer and recommending the firm as a good place to work and conduct business. The tremendous cost of turnover — ranging from six to 18 months of an employees' salary — should signal to managers the need to get a return on investment from the recruitment/selection process, as well as recognize the time, energy, effort and money spent tending to the applicant who was hired (and for the other applications who were not hired).

New employees are important to the organization because their ideas and ways of work may challenge company paradigms and culture. In ambitious new hires and/or more seasoned talent, there may be a desire among these individuals to make their mark or change things quickly without realizing unintended consequences or inertia of the company. Therefore, if a new hire came to the company with unreasonable expectations, this new employee will more quickly self-select out of the company. Managers and peers can play a large role in managing and shaping expectations, and in providing a welcoming environment that is inclusive of diverse perspectives and new ideas.

Another reason new employees are important is the often significant effect these employees have on customer service, loyalty and relationships. Many front-line employees have interactions with customers and may be the public face of the business. In fact, 90 percent of contact that customers have with companies is with the least trained group: front-line employees. Thus, it is important that turnover be minimized to the extent possible given industry and occupation norms, and that managers provide adequate training, pay a fair wage and follow through on promises made during the recruitment/selection process. Otherwise, negative reactions from new front-line employees may adversely affect customer relationships.

What We Know About *New Employees* and Engagement

The numbers are staggering: Nearly 1-in-4 workers has been with his/her employer less than 12 months, and more than one-third of employees have been with their employer less than two years. In fact, more employees have tenure of less than two years than have tenure of 10 years or more.

Although there is a correlation between the age of the employee and tenure, "new" employees cross all age ranges. (See "Tenure in 2006" on page 28.) From the analysis of the three "National Workforce Engagement Benchmark Studies," two work factors have the strongest impact on the engagement of employees to the organization: "daily satisfaction" and "ethics, diversity and safety."

Tenure in 2006

According to the "Tenure in 2006" report from the U.S. Bureau of Labor Statistics:

Years of Age	Tenure
16-19	Nearly 9-in-10 employees have less than two years of service with the organization (86 percent).
20-24	Nearly two-thirds of employees have less than two years of service with the organization (63 percent).
25-34	Nearly 4-in-10 employees have less than two years of service with the organization (38 percent).
35-44	1-in-4 employees has less than two years of service with the organization (25 percent).
45-54	Nearly 1-in-5 employees has less than two years of service with the organization (18 percent).
55-64	More than 1-in-7 employees have less than two years of service with the organization (15 percent).
65 or older	1-in-7 employees has less than two years of service with the organization (14 percent).

As seen in all three studies, "I have a good relationship with my immediate supervisor" is a key driver of engagement. Fully engaged employees are nearly twice as likely as unengaged employees to agree with this statement, while unengaged employees are nearly eight times more likely to disagree (23 percent versus 3 percent).

Given the amount of interaction that newer employees generally have with their supervisor, "I enjoy coming to work" is greatly affected by the relationship they have with their boss.

"Company policies are carried out in a fair and just manner" is one area directly affected by the supervisor or manager of a department, division or location. Although half of all employees agree with that statement (55 percent in 2008-09; no significant change from the previous two benchmark studies), the percentage is highest for the least tenured employees (75 percent), indicating that as employees gain more experience with their supervisors and managers, their perceptions of fairness decrease.

In addition, "I feel I am valued as an employee," another area affected by an employee's direct supervisor or manager, is a key driver of engagement and retention of these least tenured employees. Again, the perception of employees weakens as their tenure increases in the organization. While nearly three-quarters of employees with their company less than three months feel valued (74 percent), slightly less than 6-in-10 (59 percent) of 10-plus-years employees feel the same way.

Strategies to Engage *New Employees*

- Determine the job a new person is to undertake.
- Select the right person, for the right job, at the right time.
- Provide a realistic job preview.
- Orient the new employee to the organization, work team and job.
- Set challenging, yet achievable, performance expectations.
- Offer meaningful on-the-job training and encourage questions.
- Allocate appropriate tools and technology for work.

Determine the Job a New Person Is to Undertake

This requires that managers — either individually or in cooperation with HR — properly analyze the job the new employee is expected to perform. The first step in the recruitment/selection process is understanding the nature of work, including duties and responsibilities, competencies needed for success, tools and technology used to perform the job, types of decisions and reporting relationships required of the role, and typical outcomes expected. Taking time to properly understand the job for which a new employee will be hired can lead to a greater chance that the organization will select the right person, for the right job, at the right time.

Select the Right Person, for the Right Job, at the Right Time

After analyzing the job, the manager should seek to recruit the best possible candidate for employment. The methods used to recruit talent should be driven based on the nature of work, scarcity or abundance of talent in the labor market, and past practices (both successes and failures) of various recruitment methods.

Typical external recruitment methods include employee referrals, advertisements (in both general and targeted media), staffing or employment agencies, recruiters and college recruiting, among others.

After recruiting a pool of candidates, managers need to properly select talent. This usually is done through interviews, pre-employment testing, having candidates perform and/or provide work samples related to the job and other methods to gauge the fit a person has with the job and the organization.

Provide a Realistic Job Preview

It is vital that managers provide new employees with a realistic job preview during the recruitment/selection phase and the initial orientation period. This includes telling candidates and new hires both the good and bad perspectives of the job and the organization. This provides a balanced, realistic sense of the challenges, rewards and nature of how work is to be performed. Many managers tend to "oversell" the job or the organization to new employees, only to have these employees literally (and perhaps a bit naively) believe what they are told. Providing a realistic preview of the context for work, including performance expectations, helps facilitate an employee's effective orientation and integration into the organization.

Orient the New Employee to the Organization, Work Team and Job

New employees need to know vital things about their new work context, and often managers tend to overlook providing a proper orientation to the organization, work team and job. Regardless of the existence or absence of a formal orientation program through which new employees participate, it is incumbent on the manager to ensure that employees know certain vital information about the company: its mission, vision, values and strategy; the nature of products, services, customers and competitive strengths; the people and departments with whom the new employee will frequently interact; and the scope, nature and expected outcomes of the specific job.

Set Challenging, Yet Achievable, Performance Expectations

Closely related to orientation is the setting of challenging, yet achievable, performance expectations for new employees. This typically is the purview of the new employee's direct manager and, in this context, "performance management" refers to an overarching series of activities on the part of the manager — not the once a year performance-appraisal meeting.

Thus, performance management requires a manager to communicate early, often and up front to employees about the specific expectations for how work should be performed, and how the outcomes of work performance ultimately will be evaluated. Inherent in this discussion should be the sources of performance data that managers will use to evaluate performance, and the ways — both formally and informally — employees will know how well they are performing in the job.

Offer Meaningful On-the-Job Training and Encourage Questions

To equip new employees with a platform for good performance to occur, managers need to ensure that meaningful on-the-job training is provided. Regardless of the organization-, industry- or occupation-specific training a new employee receives, on-the-job training is most vital in helping new employees contextualize how their knowledge, skills and abilities will be actualized on the job. Therefore, managers should ensure that new employees are given adequate time and attention to acquire and apply learning in the context in which performance ultimately will occur.

Closely related to on-the-job training is creating a culture where asking question is encouraged. In some organizations, having a new employee asking questions may be viewed as a sign of weakness rather than as a sign of strength (e.g., new employees may feel they need to prove themselves quickly). Existing employees may feel that new employees — especially experienced ones — should already "know" certain things. Managers can help avoid these dynamics by proactively and continuously setting a culture in which asking questions is viewed positively, and where knowledge sharing is openly encouraged.

Allocate Appropriate Tools and Technology for Work

After finding, orienting and integrating new employees into the organization, work team and job, managers need to ensure their ongoing success by allocating appropriate tools and technology for work performance. Access to reasonable physical, financial, human, intellectual and technological resources is one tangible way a manager can signal his/her commitment to the new employee's success. This also is one area of a new employee's work over which the manager has significant control and can help reinforce that he/she has the new employee's best interests in mind. Allocation of these resources, of course, implies that managers have a firm understanding of the job a new employee is to undertake.

Action Planning Log for Engaging *New Employees*

Employee Name	Specific Actions Planned to Engage Employee

What is the organization doing especially well to engage *New Employees*?

In what ways can the organization improve its efforts to engage *New Employees*?

chapter 3
ENGAGING MID-CAREER EMPLOYEES

Who are *Mid-Career Employees,* and Why Are They Important?

Mid-career employees are those individuals who typically have been in the organization for three to five years. These individuals often are viewed as the "worker bees" — those who generally are proficient in accomplishing the work of the company. As a result, these employees may easily blend into the fabric of the organization; managers may take their ongoing commitment to the company for granted.

Ironically, these same employees may have reached a plateau in their jobs, and may be looking outside the organization for new challenges and opportunities for advancement. These employees likely are "headhunter-ready" because of their experience, knowledge and demonstrated performance track record. Therefore, it is vital that managers be aware of why mid-career employees are important, and how to go about enhancing their engagement.

Mid-career employees are important resources for any organization, simply given the sheer amount of time, money, management and development that companies have invested into these employees. After three to five years in an organization, mid-career employees have acquired specialized knowledge, skills and experiences, their network of relationships is increased and, ironically, the company may have inadvertently trained the employee to leave. At this stage of their employment, many mid-career employees are at a juncture in deciding whether the job and organization is more of a "short-term transaction" or a "long-term relationship" — and how managers handle these employees could drive them away or deepen their organizational commitment.

Many mid-career employees may not get the attention of their managers on a regular basis. New employees and underperforming employees tend to receive the most intensive interventions from managers, and often the steady performing mid-career employee is taken for granted, back-burnered in terms of communication, feedback or training, and may not be a top priority for managers.

From a succession planning and "promotability" standpoint, mid-career employees represent an important talent management pipeline to the organization. These employees are poised to become vital as the next group of leaders. As a result, cross-training and leadership development issues are critical. This is especially true in industries where the vast majority of senior-level employees are retiring or leaving and for industries in which talent attraction is a challenging endeavor.

Finally, mid-career employees may get "comfortable" in the job, and the initial excitement they held as new employees may have worn off ("It's just a job, not an adventure"). Some of these individuals are literally stuck in a rut: They may still want to work for the organization, but may feel boxed in and frustrated at their inability to advance or move around the organization. Alternatively, mid-career employees may become trapped for one of three reasons. These employees may:

- Have golden handcuffs, the situation in which financial and other aspects of work make it difficult for the employee to replicate the employment situation elsewhere.
- Feel they lack the skills necessary to find other jobs outside the organization.
- Feel otherwise qualified and comfortable with their skill set, yet do not believe there are other external jobs available to them.

What We Know About *Mid-Career Employees* and Engagement

One in six employees has been with his/her organization three to five years. This number increases to 1-in-4 employees who are between 25 and 34 years of age. According to the "2008-09 National Workforce Engagement Benchmark Study," 41 percent of three- to five-year tenured employees are fully engaged with their organization, while 35 percent feel unengaged — slightly worse than 2004-05 and 2006-07. These employees are no less reluctant (either reluctant to leave or to work hard) than other tenured groups, indicating they have choice and don't necessarily feel trapped in their jobs.

The perceptions employees have about their immediate supervisor or manager decrease as their tenure increases. In other words, as employees gain experience with their boss, their thoughts and feelings worsen. (See "Supervisor Index.")

Roughly 30 percent of employees who have been with the organization for less than five years have a positive perception of their relationship with their boss, a significant decline from 2006-07 levels. Of greater concern, three- to five-

Supervisor Index

Tenure	Supervisor Index
Less than 90 days' tenure	3.8
90 days' to one year tenure	3.6
Two years' tenure	3.5
Three years' tenure	3.4
Six-plus years' tenure	3.5
2008-09 Overall Benchmark	3.5

Note: Based on a five-point scale, with 5 equaling "strongly agree" and 1 equaling "strongly disagree."

year tenured employees are three times more likely to feel negatively about their relationship with their supervisor than brand new employees (23 percent negative versus 8 percent negative).

From the analysis of the national benchmark, five work factors have the most impact on the engagement of these three- to five-year tenured employees to the organization (in order of importance):

- Daily satisfaction
- Reputation management
- Ethics, diversity and safety
- Effective senior leadership
- Training and development.

As discussed earlier in this chapter, three- to five-year employees expect the opportunity for learning and development inside the organization and look for advancement possibilities to further their careers. With slightly more than 4-in-10 of these employees fully engaged, it's not surprising the perceptions of employees are so negative. In 2008-09:

- Just 6-in-10 of all three- to five-year tenured employees feel their performance on the job is fairly judged (59 percent), the same as in 2006-07.
- Less than half feel that qualified employees usually are allowed to transfer to a better job (49 percent), a significant decrease from 2006-07 levels.
- Half feel their organization provides opportunities for advancement (51 percent).
- Less than half feel their organization does a good job of supporting employee career development (45 percent), a decrease from 2006-07 levels.
- Less than half feel they have opportunities for promotion within their division or department (45 percent), slightly worse than in 2006-07.

With regard to "training and development," the picture from the 2008-09 national benchmark is even worse. Note that three- to five-year tenured employees agree with the following:

- "This organization provides training and development that supports short- and long-term career objectives." (52 percent)
- "This organization is interested in helping me achieve my long-term career objectives." (39 percent) This is a decline from 2006-07 ratings.
- "I regularly attend training programs/courses related to my job." (40 percent) This is slightly better than the 38 percent of three- to five-year workers who attended training programs in 2006-07.

It is understandable that supervisors would be reticent in providing training and development and advancement opportunities to their staffs. In most cases, supervisors are rated, paid and given bonuses on some measure of the "productivity" of their staff. If supervisors approve the transfer of one of their most productive employees, their own performance (as judged by the performance of their staff) will decrease. Even though this transfer may be a good decision for the organization, *everyone is the CEO of one organization, and that one organization is themselves.*

If supervisors or managers are negatively affected by a transfer or promotion of one of their staff, the transfer will never happen. For supervisors and managers to act differently, they need to be incented differently, as well. Thus, as an organization, it is important to *train your employees so they can leave, or else they'll leave.*

Strategies to Engage *Mid-Career Employees*

- Re-energize employees through job enlargement, enrichment and rotation.
- Provide movement upward, laterally and, in some cases, externally.
- Invest in more long-term, career-oriented training.
- Recognize that company reputation becomes more important to employees.
- Manage performance in a more holistic, developmentally focused manner.
- Identify and use employees as mentors for new and underperforming employees.
- Connect high-potential employees to superstar and/or long-term employees.
- Discuss with employees their continued "fit" with the job, work team and organization.

Re-energize Employees Through Job Enlargement, Enrichment and Rotation

Job enlargement involves giving the job incumbent additional duties that require the same level of skill, effort or responsibility as those currently performed. The additional duties should be a natural outgrowth of current duties, and enlarging a job permits an employee to learn additional skills and become cross-trained on other functions.

Job enrichment provides additional duties that require more complex levels of skill, effort or responsibility as those currently performed. Enriching a job permits an employee to acquire higher-level skills, permits the supervisor to determine whether the employee is a candidate for promotion, and can aid in succession planning.

Finally, job rotation involves giving the job incumbent additional duties that require different levels of skill, effort or responsibility as those currently performed. Rotated jobs should relate, in some manner, to the current job. Rotating jobs permits an employee to increase his/her skills, develop a big-picture perspective, alleviate boredom from performing the same job and add greater value to the organization.

Provide Movement Upward, Laterally and, in Some Cases, Externally

When one ponders advancement opportunities at work, moving up in an organization's hierarchy generally is the direction considered most desirable. Historically, the most common form of advancement was climbing the career ladder in a traditional, hierarchical organizational structure. Upward mobility via advancement is still widespread, and several organizations actively adopt a "promote from within" philosophy to staffing decisions.

Unlike moving up, moving around refers to lateral moves that afford employees with the opportunities to increase their value to the organization by acquiring additional knowledge, skills, experiences and competencies. Lateral moves have become a more common form of "advancement" in the past two decades, largely because flattened organizational structures have limited hierarchically upward moves.

Sometimes, opportunities for advancement require an employee to leave the present employment situation. While turnover is a concern to any employer, the fact remains that it is impossible, impractical and even undesirable to retain every employee. Moving out recognizes that, for a variety of reasons, an employee may voluntarily elect to leave the organization.

Invest in More Long-Term, Career-Oriented Training

Because mid-career employees are poised to have leadership potential and also may be deepening their relationship with the organization, it makes sense for managers to invest in more long-term, career-oriented training for these employees. While recognizing that career development is, ultimately, the responsibility of the individual (and not the organization), managers can and should ensure that mid-career employees take advantage of training opportunities that provide them a platform of skills to move up, move around and, as noted, move out of the organization in some cases. At this stage of the employment life cycle, managers should be more concerned with the mid-career employee's ongoing fit with the organization versus the initial job for which he/she was hired.

Recognize That Company Reputation Becomes More Important to Employees

After investing time, energy and effort for three to five years, mid-career employees have truly become part of the fabric that makes the organization function reasonably well. As a result, for these employees in particular, company reputation becomes more important. How the organization is viewed in the community and industry is a direct reflection on these employees' contributions to the organization. How favorably the organization's products and services are viewed by customers can be a source of pride or, conversely, embarrassment to employees who have made a commitment to the organization. And how the organization is viewed as an employer — that is, the reputation the firm has as an attractive and desirable place to be an employee — can reinforce to these mid-career employees that their return on investment is paying off. While these reputation management issues are, of course, not within the sole purview of most managers, it is nonetheless important for managers to recognize the subtle and profound ways the organization's reputation reinforces a mid-career employee's decision and attitude about the employer.

Manage Performance in a More Holistic, Developmentally Focused Manner

Because mid-career employees likely have mastered the routine and recurring nature of their jobs, performance management should take on a more holistic, developmentally focused manner for managers. Managers still must outline and monitor performance expectations for their direct reports. However, for mid-career employees, performance management should provide stretch goals and focus on preparing employees for new or different roles in the work team or broader organization. It is, therefore, necessary and desirable that mid-career employees have more customized, diverse and challenging performance expectations, and that these performance expectations need not be the same for each mid-career employee. Managers should expect and encourage more challenging performance from mid-career employees, and should increasingly tap into these employees for leadership development and other special project roles — all with an eye toward further developing their robust capabilities for an ongoing relationship with the organization.

Identify and Use Employees as Mentors for New and Underperforming Employees

One way managers can re-energize mid-career employees is through the use of these employees as mentors for both new and underperforming employees. Because managerial time is mostly spent dealing with "the new and the bad," savvy managers realize that having an experienced, steady performing mid-career employee work with both of these groups can benefit both work-team efficiency and effectiveness.

For this arrangement to work, managers must select mid-career employees with care, and train them on the mentoring role they will occupy. Ensuring that mid-career employees have the right attitude, an adequate performance track record, an empathetic and supportive approach to mentoring employees and a willingness to take on this leadership role are all important considerations that managers must acknowledge and use in deciding whom, when and under what circumstances mid-career employees will assume these roles.

Connect High-Potential Employees to Superstar and/or Long-Term Employees

Related to mentoring of new and underperforming employees is the analogous dynamic of connecting high-potential mid-career employees to superstar and/or long-term employees for the express purpose of developing greater leadership capacity for the organization. Managers who have mid-career employees who consistently exhibit sound performance should link these employees with others in the organization who can mentor the mid-career employee to even greater levels of enhanced performance. Managers have a responsibility to help the organization develop its talent pipeline, and should seek out superstar and long-term employees from other departments or work teams to mentor mid-career employees within the manager's own portfolio.

Discuss With Employees Their Continued Fit With the Job, Work Team and Organization

Because most employees tend to stay with their organization between three and five years, it makes sense that managers initiate a discussion with mid-career employees about their continued "fit" with the job, work team and organization. Managers are in the best position to talk to employees about their own individual goals and how the employee's goals might mesh with the longer-term prospects of the organization.

Managers also are in the best position to assess the extent to which mid-career employees are meeting and exceeding performance standards, and whether these employees might be ready for new challenges and opportunities, either within or outside the organization. Ongoing discussion with mid-career employees by the manager signals to the employee that the manager is interested in his/her continued development, and might provide a venue to discuss ways to provide the employee additional engagement in the form of job enlargement, enrichment or rotation, among other considerations.

Action Planning Log for Engaging *Mid-Career Employees*

Employee Name	Specific Actions Planned to Engage Employee

What is the organization doing especially well to engage *Mid-Career Employees*?

In what ways can the organization improve its efforts to engage *Mid-Career Employees*?

chapter 4
ENGAGING UNDERPERFORMING EMPLOYEES

Who Are *Underperforming Employees,* and Why Are They Important?

As the name implies, underperforming employees are individuals who, for whatever reason, are not meeting minimum performance expectations for the job. These employees may be viewed as reluctant to perform or, in fact, may be unengaged with the job or the organization. In some cases, individuals are underperforming because of an improper fit with the job, the manager or the organization — something that, should this be a frequent occurrence, the organization would want to rectify through its enhanced recruitment and selection processes. Finally, some employees are simply "bad apples" for whom no amount of organizationally sanctioned interventions and opportunities will improve performance. In any event, managers must recognize why underperforming employees are important to the organization, along with ways to identify, develop and, in some cases, release marginal, difficult and/or improperly fit, underperforming employees.

While it might seem incongruous to pronounce that underperforming employees are important to an organization, the simple reality is that these employees are part of the organization and frequently interact with other employees, business partners, suppliers and, most notably, customers. For this reason alone, the relationship-jeopardizing behaviors that underperforming employees engage in should give managers enough concern to want to deal with these individuals.

Perhaps a more pragmatic reason for recognizing the importance of underperforming employees is the fact that these people still are expected to do minimally acceptable work for the organization. The organization has invested time, energy, effort and money in finding, training and managing these employees, so it stands to reason that managers should seek to realize a sufficient return on their investment.

Often, managers may not know how to handle underperforming employees. Most managers tend to exhibit high performance standards and/or possess leadership characteristics and qualities that are, in many cases, nearly 180 degrees away from the behaviors and attitudes of some underperforming employees. Simply put, many high-functioning managers cannot understand the mentality of underperforming employees because the managers behave in ways that tend to exhibit higher performing characteristics.

As a result, managers may not be comfortable handling underperforming employees. Often, they are not trained in how to identify, review and correct poor performance. They may be intimidated by an underperforming employee, and may not feel it is worth the effort to try to correct poor performance. In this instance, a "management-by-neglect" approach may emerge: managers do not know how to handle, are not comfortable approaching or prefer to not be bothered with underperforming employees; thus they simply hope performance will magically improve without managerial intervention.

What We Know About *Underperforming Employees* and Engagement

Realistically, underperforming employees can be "saved" depending on the desire of the organization to "keep" the employee and the employee's ability to improve his/her performance through additional training and development.

There is a very strong correlation between employee engagement and performance. Employees who do not feel "like part of the family," who don't feel that "the organization's problems are my problems too" and who do not have a "personal or psychological attachment to the company" are significantly less likely to perform above the minimum. However, an engaged employee may not have the skills, competencies or experience to perform meaningful work, just as an unengaged employee may meet or exceed the minimum requirements of a job. Therefore the level of engagement an employee feels for his/her organization is not the only determining factor in whether the employee "stays longer, works harder or recommends the organization as a great place to work," nor is it the only factor in his/her performance.

According to the "2008-09 National Workforce Engagement Benchmark Study," 43 percent of employees are fully engaged, 32 percent are unengaged and 25 percent are reluctant (reluctant to leave and/or reluctant to work hard). Although a slight improvement from 2006-07 levels, when nearly as many people were pulling for their company as were pushing against it (40 percent fully engaged and 36 percent unengaged), the 2008-09 engagement levels are still weaker than the 2004-05 levels. The findings from this third national benchmark indicate the dangers inherent when 6-in-10 employees are not actively engaged with their employers. So how does a lack of engagement translate into weaker employee performance? Consider:

- Only one-third of unengaged workers are "highly motivated to work hard," compared to 97 percent of fully engaged workers.

- Less than 60 percent of unengaged workers have a "strong desire to go the extra mile for customers," compared to 96 percent of fully engaged workers.
- Less than 1-in-12 unengaged workers would "remain at their company even if offered slightly more money to leave," compared to 92 percent of fully engaged employees. A lack of engagement can start at the recruiting phase when organizations fail to find the right talent, for the right job, at the right time.
- Four-in-ten unengaged employees agree "there is a good fit between my skills/interests and my job," while 3-in-10 disagree.

Performance problems can be exacerbated by weakness in an employer's on-boarding and orientation. In all aspects of organizational orientation, unengaged employees are six to 10 times more likely to feel negatively than fully engaged employees. (See "Feelings Toward the Organization Among Unengaged and Engaged Employees.")

A lack of training and development is another key factor in many employee performance issues. Again, unengaged employees (many of whom do not meet performance standards) feel significantly more negatively about their training and development opportunities than fully engaged workers. (See "Feelings Toward Training and Development Among Unengaged and Engaged Employees" on page 47.)

Feelings Toward the Organization Among Unengaged and Engaged Employees

National Benchmark Study Question	Unengaged Employees (Percent Disagree)	Fully Engaged Employees (Percent Disagree)
I have a clear understanding of the company's mission, vision, values and objectives, and the role I play in them.	24%	3%
I am well-informed as to how my job fits in with our total company.	25%	2%
My manager has explained the performance expectations of my job.	26%	4%
The company provides me the information I need to make good decisions.	28%	3%

Feelings Toward Training and Development Among Unengaged and Engaged Employees

National Benchmark Study Question	Unengaged Employees (Percent Agree)	Fully Engaged Employees (Percent Agree)
I believe this organization provides training and development that supports short- and long-term objectives.	27%	73%
I am provided with sufficient training to perform my job to the best of my ability.	31%	80%
The quality of my orientation and training received for my current position was satisfactory.	28%	78%
I regularly attend training programs/courses related to my job.	19%	58%

Performance problems begin when companies "hire" instead of recruit, neglect to provide adequate training and development to employees for their current job, disregard ensuring the best employees receive the greatest rewards, and put retention before engagement. Thus, when organizations recruit, retrain, reward and retain their employees, performance problems can be avoided — or overcome.

Strategies to Engage *Underperforming Employees*

- Identify the underperforming employee.
- Determine if performance deficiency is knowledge-/skill-related or attitude-/motivation-related.
- Resist the urge to simply transfer the employee to another department.
- Develop coordinated, appropriate interventions, along with expectations, metrics and timetables for success.
- Document performance and follow a progressive-discipline framework.
- Practice the adage "fire fast, hire slow."

Identify the Underperforming Employee

One of the first things managers should do when confronted with an underperforming employee is assess the nature of when underperformance is occurring. The "when" involves determining at what point or stage of the employment life cycle underperformance is identified: a new employee, a mid-career employee, a long-term employee or a former superstar employee?

Closely related to the identification of where the employee is in the life cycle is the question of whether the manager wants to keep the employee or let him/her go. Often, the longer an employee has been with an organization, the more willing the organization is to work with an underperforming employee.

Determine if Performance Deficiency Is Knowledge-/Skill-Related or Attitude-/Motivation-Related

If an employee's underperformance is due to a lack of knowledge/skill, there might be several reasons. First, the employee may not have been properly recruited and selected to the job and organization. Second, the employee may have received poor or insufficient training for the job. Third, subtle changes to the nature of work over time may have occurred, and the employee failed to keep up with such changes. Finally, managers may not have allocated appropriate tools, technology, time or training to the employee to permit the employee to maintain minimum performance proficiency. In each of these situations, there are a series of interventions managers can choose from to facilitate improved performance, ranging from tightening recruitment/selection processes for subsequent hires to retraining employees to providing reasonable resources to the employee for improved job performance.

If an employee's poor performance is attitude-/motivation-related, however, managers may be limited in terms of the explicit interventions that can be afforded. While the manager can create a context for positive attitudes and motivation to occur, ultimately employees with poor attitudes or lack of motivation must own their feelings and subsequent behaviors.

Resist the Urge to Simply Transfer the Employee to Another Department

One of the most common temptations managers have when dealing with underperforming employees it to transfer the employee to another department and expect performance to magically improve. This rarely results in performance improvement, especially if root-cause issues are not identified and addressed.

While it may be true that some employees may flourish in a new context, simply transferring employees who are underperforming to another department signals to all employees a lack of management fortitude in dealing with the problem, and may jeopardize relationships between managers who may feel as if their colleagues are undermining the collective organization's performance by not dealing with underperforming employees more directly and effectively.

Develop Coordinated, Appropriate Interventions, Along with Expectations, Metrics and Timetables for Success

Because managers must be held responsible for the actions of their employees (including underperforming employees), performance management approaches and interventions should be coordinated with others in the organization. In settings where a formal HR function exists, tapping into the expertise of this group is encouraged to ensure consistency among and between employees. In organizations without a formal HR presence, having senior management awareness, buy-in and support for performance management interventions is needed to present a unified front.

For interventions to be effective, managers should discuss with employees the nature of underperformance, elicit from the employee a reason for the underperformance, outline expectations for minimum standards of performance, create metrics of how subsequent performance will be evaluated, and develop timetables for success. Inherent in this process is the willingness of the employee to want to improve his/her performance, and the ability of a manger to stay the course in seeking to correct the performance.

Document Performance and Follow a Progressive-Discipline Framework

In all instances in which managers meet with employees to discuss performance, managers should document performance meetings to provide a legally defensible basis for their actions. Managing underperforming employees should occur under the auspices of the organization's progressive-discipline framework. ("Progressive discipline" is a series of increasingly serious oral and written warnings to facilitate the employee's removal from the organization and, in order to provide the employee a reasonable chance to correct his/her performance, managers are encouraged to use a consistent, documentable approach to progressive discipline in managing the issues surrounding underperforming employees.)

Practice the Adage "Fire Fast, Hire Slow"

Managers, employees and the organization as a whole benefit when underperforming employees recognize the nature of their performance deficiencies and take concrete steps to improve performance. There are times, however, when all of the well-intentioned and organizationally sanctioned efforts on the part of managers result in continued poor performance of underperforming employees. In many instances, such underperformance could have been avoided had the organization spent greater care and attention in outlining hiring criteria and competencies, and taking its time in the hiring process. Additionally, many organizations let poor performers become repeat offenders too many times, without ultimately making a decision to fire them until well after the time when performance should have improved. While employees should be treated with dignity and respect, including being given the time to improve their performance, quickly firing a clear under-performer — especially one with a poor attitude/motivation — is often the most desirous course of action an organization can and should pursue.

Action Planning Log for Engaging *Underperforming Employees*

Employee Name	Specific Actions Planned to Engage Employee

What is the organization doing especially well to engage
Underperforming Employees?

In what ways can the organization improve its efforts to engage
Underperforming Employees?

chapter 5
ENGAGING SUPERSTAR EMPLOYEES

Who Are *Superstar Employees,* and Why Are They Important?

The opposite of underperforming employees, superstar employees are truly top-grade talent in any organization. In some cases, these are the 20 percent of the individuals who are responsible for 80 percent of the organization's accomplishments. Superstar employees usually are high-achieving individuals who can, in many instances, be role models to other employees, and often emerge as potential leaders within the organization. They tend to be highly valued by their organizations for their ability to produce high quality work in a fairly quick fashion. These superstar employees also are, not surprisingly, the most desirable for rival employers to "steal" from the organization. Thus, it is necessary for managers to know why these employees are important, and some specific strategies to engage them more fully in the company.

Employees who hold the "superstar" title tend to have this honor bestowed upon them due to their demonstrated productivity, first and foremost. These are the types of employees who can be counted on to exceed customer expectations, and often will go above and beyond the call of duty to ensure that productivity and performance are realized. These same employees tend to be willing to take on new initiatives and often can be counted on to model the behaviors that the organization desires. Because of their energy, drive and dedication, superstar employees tend to add vitality to the group and can be a source of pride and inspiration for managers and employees alike.

In spite of the seemingly positive traits and characteristics of superstar employees, there are some potentially challenging circumstances involved in managing these types of employees. Superstars may be difficult to manage and rein in, especially when they may be more technically proficient at their jobs than the manager. Some superstars foreground their own individual performance and emphasize their own accomplishments, thereby serving as a de facto "demotivator" of other staff. Superstar employees may also tend to be loners and "worker bees," and may not necessarily be good managers as a result of their emphasis on pride of individual accomplishment.

Organizations may inadvertently reward superstar outcomes without considering the behaviors and processes superstars use to achieve performance. The ends-justifies-the-means mentality of rewarding superstar performance may place such performance at odds with collaborative styles and ethical work cultures. In some cases, superstar employees may demonstrate blunt, assertive, aggressive or ambitious behaviors — traits that can be strengths in some contexts and liabilities in others.

What We Know About *Superstar Employees* and Engagement

Many companies struggle to keep their most critical employees engaged in the work they do. Just as gifted children need to be continually challenged to avoid boredom, it's the same principle with gifted (superstar) employees.

For most companies today, 80 percent of the organization's revenue comes from 20 percent of the customers. This also is known as the Pareto Principle. This same principle applies to many working situations, in which 80 percent of the work is performed by 20 percent of the employees. There are five areas that supervisors must address for organizations to hang on to their superstar employees, who are, in many cases, their critical staff:

• Daily satisfaction
• Training and development
• Rewards and recognition
• Tools and technology
• Opportunities for advancement.

According to the "2008-09 National Workforce Engagement Benchmark Study," there certainly is room for improvement in these areas. Although there is a new designation in the 2008-09 national benchmark for "superstar" employees, it is self-described. The authors believe employers do, in fact, treat these critical employees better than employees who may not be as vital. Therefore, the perceptions of superstar employees would be slightly higher, as is evidenced in the current benchmark results:

• Nearly 7-in-10 employees (69 percent) agree that their job "provides me a feeling of personal accomplishment and there is a good fit between my skills and abilities and my job." These ratings are more positive than 2006-07 ratings, but worse than the 2004 ratings, when 72 percent agreed.
• Nearly two-thirds of all employees (64 percent) agree they "have the opportunity to learn new skills." However 1-in-6 (16 percent) disagree.
• More than half of all employees (54 percent) agree that their organization

"provides training and development that supports short- and long-term career objectives," an improvement from 2006-07 levels (49 percent) and at parity with 2004-05 results.

- Four-in-ten employees (44 percent) agree their organization is "interested in helping me achieve my long-term career objectives."
- Just 4-in-10 employees (42 percent) agree they "regularly attend training programs/courses related to my job;" however, one-third of all employees disagree with the statement (33 percent). These ratings are slightly better than 2006-07 benchmark results, but worse than the ratings in the original 2004-05 study.

There were significant improvements among employees in two areas related to rewards and recognition from the 2004-05 and 2006-07 benchmark results:

- "People are fairly rewarded and recognized for their contributions to the company's success and excellent performance gets rewarded at this organization." (48 percent of superstars agree; 30 percent disagree.)
- "My manager ensures that the best (employees) receive the greatest rewards and recognition." (42 percent of superstars agree; 29 percent disagree.)

Superstar employees often expect a higher level of autonomy from their boss than do other workers:

- Seventy-three percent of all employees agree they are given "enough authority to get their job done."
- Seventy-three percent of employees believe they have "the freedom to make their own decisions at work," while 1-in-6 disagree (10 percent), significant improvements from both 2006-07 and 2004-05 levels.
- Just half of all employees (53 percent) are "encouraged to try new ways of doing things at work," while 1-in-5 (20 percent) disagree, no change from 2006-07 and significantly worse than 2004-05 results.

Finally, just more than half of all employees agree their organization "provides opportunities for advancement" (52 percent), while nearly 1-in-4 employees disagree (23 percent), and less than half agree their company "does a good job supporting employee career development" (49 percent). These results reflect no change from the two previous benchmark efforts.

In the 2008-09 benchmark, employees were asked if they truly considered themselves a superstar. Although there is no way to verify whether the employer agrees with the categorization, the results are nonetheless intriguing:

- Fifty percent of superstar employees are fully engaged, compared to 32 percent of those not self-described as a superstar.

- Only 25 percent of superstars are unengaged, compared to 43 percent of nonsuperstars. It is worth noting that individuals may still consider themselves superstars — based on their own intrinsic sense of self, work ethic, etc. — even though the organizational context in which they work is not as engaging to them as employees.

In 2008-09, self-reported superstars are significantly:

- More positive in their perceptions of supervision, communications and fairness
- More likely to stay longer, work harder, and recommend the organization as a great place to work
- More positive about every aspect of their competitive assessment of their job as it relates to other employees with similar jobs at other companies (e.g., pay, benefits, stress level, work-life balance, relationship with supervisor, relationship with co-workers, training and development, and opportunities for advancement).
- More positive in every single item in the 13 components of workforce engagement.

Superstar employees need to be challenged in a good way, given opportunities to learn new things and improve their skills, and rewarded and recognized better than their peers. Whether a superstar is designated as such by supervisors or managers, or is more self-described, these employees are significantly more likely to go the extra mile for customers, thereby ensuring company success.

Strategies to Engage *Superstar Employees*

- Recognize that these employees tend to make decisions faster, and expect results accordingly.
- Link pay and performance more explicitly.
- Provide other intangible rewards and recognition.
- Fast-track superstar employees for training, promotion and other opportunities.
- Avoid letting an otherwise well-intentioned and good company policy stand in the way of engaging superstars.
- Effectively manage the manager-employee roles and relationships.

Recognize That These Employees Tend to Make Decisions Faster, and Expect Results Accordingly

One benefit of superstar employee behaviors is their emphasis on performance and productivity. Because superstars like to see tangible results from their own work product, so too do they expect results from those around them — including their boss. Most superstar employees operate with a heightened sense of ambition and drive, and they want those traits and characteristics valued and recognized, even by managers who may not necessarily possess those exact qualities themselves. Because of this, managers are advised to recognize that superstar employees' decision-making timeline typically is faster than a more traditional employee, and the superstar may want managerial action on important (to the superstar, at least) decisions faster than is the norm.

Closely related to this is a results orientation that places a premium on speed, efficiency and effectiveness. Superstar employees may have high expectations that results will be achieved in a short time, and may tend to articulate their frustrations when organizational activities and initiatives seem to be taking too long for the superstar's liking. Managers should work with superstars to identify and prioritize decisions and expected results while honoring the organization's decision-making culture and constraints and simultaneously respecting the superstar's inherent desire for positive action. Realistic expectation management, combined with an understanding and appreciation of the superstar's viewpoint and energy level, can go a long way toward facilitating positive management-superstar employee relations.

Link Pay and Performance More Explicitly

Perhaps more than any other type of employee, superstars tend to want their performance to be explicitly rewarded in specific, tangible ways. This necessarily extends to pay, in which superstar employees express a desire to have pay and performance linked in ways that recognize the extraordinary efforts superstars put into performing their jobs. In production-oriented environments, where outcomes of work are more explicitly observable and measurable, linking pay and performance should be easier for managers. In contexts where such observable and measurable production isn't as likely, identifying the contributions, impact and results made by superstars may be a bit more challenging. Managers should find ways to provide bonuses, incentive compensation and other forms of merit recognition to superstars while still working within prescribed organizational norms for pay and performance.

The organization's ability and willingness to pay superstar talent a premium rate may be subject to numerous criteria, conditions and constraints. However, managers recognize that an explicit link between pay and performance is something most superstar employees scrutinize, perhaps more carefully than do traditionally performing employees. Because superstars are, indeed, prime employees for rival firms to attract or steal, managers should try to explicitly reward superstar performance in ways that signal to the employee his/her value to the company.

Provide Other Intangible Rewards and Recognition

Beyond cash compensation, superstar employees also value intangible rewards and recognition, and managers of superstars should seek to identify and provide these things. Intangible rewards could include greater discretion and control over work, the ability to choose certain work assignments, greater input in decision-making, and increased scope of authority over how, when and where work is performed. Formal recognition of a job well done is highly valued by superstars, and managers often are challenged to "spread the wealth around" among superstars and other consistently reliable employees.

Beyond formal recognition, superstar employees also tend to appreciate the informal nature of recognition, such as the manager's explicit and continuous feedback on a job well done. Because many superstars have a high need for achievement, managers are advised to find ways to reward and recognize work in authentic, meaningful and customizable ways to their superstar employees.

Fast-Track Superstar Employees for Training, Promotion and Other Opportunities

In addition to rewards and recognition, superstar employees often are ripe for development opportunities, such as training, promotions and other special projects that tap into their talent, drive and energy level. Managers can signal to superstar employees their value to the organization by explicitly fast-tracking such employees for plum assignments, specialized training, leadership development opportunities and other ways that provide visibility of the superstar employee to others in the organization. Managers can be advocates for superstar employees by recommending the employee to other managers and senior leaders, and by publicly praising the work of the superstar to important internal and external stakeholders.

Job enlargement, enrichment and rotation, noted as an appropriate intervention for mid-career employees, also are excellent techniques for superstar employees. The goal is to keep superstar employees connected to the organization by deepening the affective commitment such talented employees have with the company. One way of doing that, of course, is by having the manager customize opportunities that harness the superstar employee's knowledge, skills and competencies in ways that are valuable to both the organization and the individual employee.

Avoid Letting an Otherwise Well-Intentioned and Good Company Policy Stand in the Way of Engaging Superstars

Every organization has a set of policies, practices and procedures designed to guide and shape employee behavior while simultaneously providing a reasonable degree of stability for the workplace. While necessary for the majority of employees, managers should avoid letting an otherwise well-intentioned and good company policy stand in the way of fully engaging a superstar employee.

For example, many firms require that employees stay in their job for a prescribed minimum time period (six months to one year) before transferring to another department or being eligible for promotion. For superstar talent, such policies may drive the employee out of the organization, especially given the faster decision-making timeline, discussed earlier, under which superstar employees operate. Thus, managers are encouraged to find ways to honor the "spirit of the law" with respect to their organization's policies, practices and procedures, without slavish adherence to the "letter of the law" when it comes to operating in the best interests of superstar employees and their potential in the company.

In some cases, it might make sense to relax, suspend or modify a policy to accommodate and capitalize on the unique strengths and opportunities a superstar employee offers. To do otherwise might signal to the superstar inflexibility on the part of the organization that causes the employee to question whether an ongoing commitment to this particular workplace is advisable — especially given the likelihood of the superstar's high degree of attractiveness and viability in the labor market.

Effectively Manage the Manager-Employee Roles and Relationships

As noted, superstar employees work in exceptional ways that deliver performance and productivity to many organizational settings. The challenge for managers — which represents the flip side of managing underperforming employees — is knowing how to strike the right balance between control/authority and flexibility/autonomy with respect to superstar employees. Selfless managers, those secure in their own knowledge, track record and accomplishments, often are best at managing superstar employees and serving as a powerful advocate for their retention and advancement in the organization. Insecure, power-hungry, myopically focused managers, on the other hand, may feel threatened by superstar employees and want to squash some of their opportunities.

Senior leaders should encourage managers to act in ways that benefit the organization as a whole, and should reward managers for developing and deploying superstar talent beyond a manager's own department or work team. For their part, managers should recognize the unique nature of superstar employee behaviors, dispositions and work orientations, and find ways to manage this dynamic employee against the desire to treat all employees consistently.

Action Planning Log for Engaging *Superstar Employees*

Employee Name	Specific Actions Planned to Engage Employee

What is the organization doing especially well to engage *Superstar Employees*?

In what ways can the organization improve its efforts to engage *Superstar Employees*?

chapter 6
ENGAGING RETURNING EMPLOYEES

Who Are *Returning Employees,* and Why Are They Important?

Perhaps you can go home again. Returning employees represent those individuals who, for one reason or another, voluntarily left the organization (instead of being fired) to pursue a personal, academic or professional interest elsewhere, and are now rejoining the organization. Sometimes, employees leave for greener pastures, only to discover that the grass wasn't so green on the other side of the fence. Some employees leave to pursue a vocation, hobby or academic endeavor, only to return to the organization at a later date. And, of course, some employees simply make a mistake in leaving, and want to return to the organization as quickly as possible and pick right back up where they left off.

Regardless of the reason for leaving or wanting to come back, returning employees do offer several advantages to employers. First, these employees can often hit the ground running, and may have even picked up new or enhanced skills in their time away from the organization. Second, the startup costs may be less because there might be few to no rehire costs. Also, investment in training and development may similarly be less than a brand-new hire, especially if the employee is coming back to a similar job. Third, a returning employee may "evangelize" the organization as a good place to work, and existing employees may also see the organization in a new light (e.g., "The person left and came back, so this place must be pretty good."). This leads to a good public relations moment for the organization, which can be viewed as forgiving of an employee's decision to leave, and can enhance the organization's reputation because returning employees can become strong internal advocates for the organization. Finally, and most saliently from an employee engagement standpoint, returning employees are likely to stay twice as long as they initially did, something that should signal to managers a sound reason for giving a returning employee another chance.

In spite of these positive considerations for rehiring a former employee, there are some potential drawbacks to returning employees. First, past behavior is a good indication of future behavior, and returning individuals have already shown a predisposition to leave the organization once. Even though they are likely to stay twice as long the second time around, there exists the chance that employees will simply leave again if they perceive their needs aren't being met. Second, co-workers and customers will give returning employees less latitude to make errors as they would a new employee, especially if the co-workers and customers have had prior experience with the returning employee. In essence, the honeymoon period is shortened considerably. Finally, returning employees may be viewed by existing employees as "disloyal" to the organization. Further complicating this dynamic are the circumstances under which the returning employee is either promoted or treated better (in terms of better pay, position, schedule, opportunities, etc.). Existing employees may perceive that their "loyalty" is not as valued and may adopt a "me too" strategy of leaving and then hoping to return.

What We Know About *Returning Employees* and Engagement

The key to engaging returning employees is determining the reasons the employee left in the first place. According to Leigh Branham, author of *The 7 Hidden Reasons Employees Leave*:

- Job or workplace was not as expected
- Mismatch between job and the person
- Too little coaching and feedback
- Too few growth and advancement opportunities
- Feeling devalued and unrecognized
- Stress from overwork and work-life imbalance
- Loss of trust and confidence in senior leaders.

What isn't on the list? Money. No matter what you read on the exit interview, money is a satisfier, not a driver of workforce engagement.

All too frequently, employers will oversell a job to an applicant or not talk about any problems the company is facing in order to fill the position. Unfortunately, it becomes obvious to the new hire that things aren't what they were touted to be, and that causes dissatisfaction and mistrust. In terms of "boomerang" employees, this is less of a concern, as the returning employee will not have any of the illusions that might have been a cause of them leaving in the first place. They know the job and the company.

In addition, there needs to be a good fit between the skills and interests of the returning employee. However the data from the "2008-09 National Workforce Engagement Benchmark Study" paints a disturbing picture that has not improved in five years. Only 7-in-10 employees agree with the following:

- "My job is satisfying to me." (70 percent)
- "My job provides me a feeling of personal accomplishment." (69 percent)
- "There is a good fit between my skills/interests and the job." (70 percent)

Often times, excellent employees leave because they don't get the feedback and coaching they want on a consistent basis. Only 7-in-10 employees (69 percent) agree their manager has explained the performance expectations of the job, while 6-in-10 employees (62 percent) believe their performance is judged fairly and their supervisor gives clearly defined performance goals and objectives (60 percent).

The No. 1 reason people stay with their companies has to do with development opportunities, not salary. Excellent employees want and expect to have advancement opportunities, especially if they are returning. The average employee has tenure of four years with his/her organization before finding another job. Nearly one-quarter of these employees (23 percent) do not feel their organization provides opportunities for advancement, while 31 percent of six- to nine-year tenured employees share the same concern. If these employees leave and then are interested in coming back, the organization needs to agree there will be advancement opportunities for the returning employee in the future.

More than 4-in-10 employees agree that employee loyalty is appropriately valued and rewarded at their company (45 percent), believe senior leadership treats employees like their most important asset (43 percent), and believe their manager ensures that the best employees receive the greatest rewards and recognition (42 percent), all significant improvements from 2006-07. However 6-in-10 employees can't agree with those statements. If good employees left their organization because they didn't feel they were being adequately rewarded for their contributions to the company's success, the situation has to be rectified before the employee comes back.

As Leigh Branham mentions in her book, "when you force workers into choosing between having a life and a career, your organization has a toxic culture." Today, only 56 percent of all employees agree that "managers recognize the importance of your personal and family life." If you make employees choose between work and life, more often than not they will choose life. If this is the reason employees left in the first place, and the organizational culture does not change to embrace work-life balance, the returning employee surely will leave again.

Finally, senior leadership can have a major impact on employees leaving — or wanting to come back. Today, less than 6-in-10 employees agree their company's senior leadership is effective (56 percent), agree the senior management has a clear vision for the future of the company (53 percent), are satisfied with the strategic direction of the company (60 percent), and believe senior leaders are people of high personal integrity (53 percent). All show significant improvement from 2006-07 levels; however, the adage "employees quit a boss, not a company" pertains to senior leadership as well.

Strategies to Engage *Returning Employees*

- Identify reasons why employees initially left and their motives for returning.
- Assess the organization's willingness and ability to accommodate returning employees' needs and expectations.
- Ensure that returning employees are informed of any changes to organizational strategy, policies and procedures.
- Handle special concerns or considerations related to a returning employee.
- Evaluate the long-term effectiveness of providing options and opportunities to returning employees.

Identify Reasons Why Employees Initially Left and Their Motives for Returning

In considering whether to rehire a former employee, smart managers must first identify reasons why employees initially left the organization, as well as their motives for wanting to return. If the returning employee was a former direct report of the manager, this identification and determination is perhaps easier because, presumably, the manager recalls why the employee left. In instances when returning employees did not previously work under the purview of the hiring manager, the new manager must make an effort to determine why the employee initially left. Sources of this information are the returning employee, his/her former manager and colleagues, HR professionals and related documents (e.g., exit interviews, performance appraisals). Obviously, great care, discretion, sensitivity and professionalism must be undertaken on the part of the manager when checking internal references on a returning employee. Managers hiring returning employees also will want to identify the motives for an employee's return, and determine if they align with the organization's best interests. This involves assessing the organization's willingness and ability to accommodate returning employees' needs and expectations.

Assess the Organization's Willingness and Ability to Accommodate Returning Employees' Needs and Expectations

Organizational philosophies vary on whether rehiring former employees is permitted. In rigid systems, companies have "no rehire" policies, presumably to engender employee loyalty. In other settings, decisions to rehire former employees are based on the unique situation and characteristics of the individual employee who seeks to return. Progressive employers even maintain an "alumni" program where they keep in contact (electronically and through current employees) to keep former employees in the loop on organizational initiatives — for the express purpose of reaching out to key individuals who are lapsed talent in the hopes of one day luring them back to the company. Additionally, many organizations permit employees to return if they are "eligible for rehire" — an often ambiguous phrase that typically means employees exercised good stewardship of their prior employment experience, including providing and working out a leave notice. Employees eligible for rehire also exhibited minimally acceptable performance standards when they were previously under the employ of the organization.

As managers assess the organization's willingness and ability to accommodate returning employees from its own perspective, they also should consider the needs and expectations returning employees now hold about their future role. Because employees tend to quit a boss and not a job, it is important for the reasons why a returning employee initially left to be identified, understood and corrected, as feasible. Albert Einstein said that the definition of insanity is doing the same thing over and over again and expecting different results. Thus, managers need to ensure that the job, relationship and other organizationally controllable variables for returning employees now align with the espoused needs and expectations of the employee. Otherwise, the returning employee's engagement likely will meet the same fate the second time around.

Ensure That Returning Employees Are Informed of Any Changes to Organizational Strategy, Policies and Procedures

Depending on the lapse of time between when a returning employee was last employed with the organization, managers may find it necessary to reorient the returning employee much in the same manner as the organization treats new employees (discussed in Chapter 2). Because organizations are dynamic and evolve to meet changing customer needs, increasing competition, evolving technologies and other pressures, the organization's strategy, including the types of products, services and solutions produced, may have radically altered since the returning employee's last affiliation. Additionally, changes to employee policies, work procedures and other aspects of the structure, culture and reporting relationships in the organization likely changed during the employee's absence. Thus, managers should not simply assume that a returning employee is completely knowledgeable and up to date on the current state of organizational affairs. This may be a bit challenging because it is natural for returning employees to assume they are, perhaps, more knowledgeable of such matters than may truly be the case. The goal, therefore, is to ensure that returning employees, like new employees, are properly indoctrinated into the organization's functioning and can hit the ground running with expediency. Nowhere is this firm understanding more critical than in situations in which a returning employee is taking on a new, maybe even more advanced, role. In this instance, managers must be equipped to handle special concerns and considerations related to this new dynamic.

Handle Special Concerns or Considerations Related to a Returning Employee

The benefits a returning employee brings to the organization — evangelizing the company as a great place to work; enhanced skills learned elsewhere; the likelihood to stay twice as long — may potentially be offset by attitudinal and other issues that existing employees hold about the returning employee. This is further compounded in situations in which the returning employee is promoted upon rehire to a supervisory, managerial or more advanced individual-contributor role. Thus, managers should be mindful of this dynamic and go to great lengths to communicate the reasons why the returning employee was selected, reminding existing employees that these individuals were held to recruitment/selection processes that likely pitted the returning employee against a competitive external applicant pool. Candid, open discussion of the potential for challenges and positive opportunities should occur. Managers of returning employees who face these situations should work with the returning employee to ensure he/she is well equipped to deal with the potential for hurt feelings or tense interpersonal relations, especially in cases in which internal talent was passed over in favor of hiring the former employee. Managers can do their part by signaling to existing employees the organization's commitment to the returning employee, and by ensuring that the decision to rehire former talent is regularly evaluated for its effectiveness in meeting individual and organizational needs.

Evaluate the Long-Term Effectiveness of Providing Options and Opportunities to Returning Employees

When returning employees rejoin an organization, both the employee and the manager give each other less time to prove or disprove the good-fit factor. The benefits of permitting returning employees to rejoin the organization must outweigh the real and perceived costs of making this opportunity available. Regularly evaluating the effectiveness of providing such options and opportunities to returning employees needs to occur. This requires managers to work with others (e.g., HR) to track the return on investment the organization achieves in rehiring lapsed talent. A few measures of success, obviously, are the retention, satisfaction and engagement exhibited by the returning employee, and this information can be gleaned from both formal means (e.g., surveying a sufficient number of returning employees at some prescribed future point) and informal methods (e.g., frequent interaction and communication between the manager and returning employee). Another measure to examine is the broader retention, satisfaction and engagement of employees who work with and, in some cases for, the returning employee. Giving employees a second chance is admirable, and often makes compelling business sense. Taking stock of the intended and unintended consequences of such practices can provide information the organization can use to shape its future staffing approaches.

Action Planning Log for Engaging *Returning Employees*

Employee Name	Specific Actions Planned to Engage Employee

What is the organization doing especially well to engage *Returning Employees*?

In what ways can the organization improve its efforts to engage *Returning Employees*?

chapter 7
ENGAGING TRANSFERRED OR PROMOTED EMPLOYEES

Who Are *Transferred or Promoted Employees,* and Why Are They Important?

In today's dynamic organizational environments, the notion of upward and lateral mobility is often the norm for many employees. Thus, transferred and promoted employees can (and do) pose challenges and rewards to managers who seek to engage them in their new roles and responsibilities. Transferred and promoted employees often are individuals who are technically proficient and have proven themselves to be knowledgeable in some organization-specific activity, product, service or solution. They also may be up-and-comers, superstars or other employees who are viewed as future leaders and for whom transfers and promotions are part of a larger, more fully articulated series of learning, growth and development opportunities. Regardless of the reason for mobility, there are several important issues managers must consider when dealing with transferred or promoted employees.

First, by transferring or promoting an individual, the organization shows that it is, indeed, interested in employee development and promoting from within. It signals to employees that the organization provides more than lip service when it comes to valuing employee contributions, as well as embodies the principle of "move up, move over or move out" that characterizes many high-performing work systems. Most significantly, transferring and promoting employees signals to all employees that, through hard work, greater success can be achieved within the organization. It does so by strengthening the intellectual capital through valuing, retaining and developing home-grown talent.

Second, because transferred and promoted employees are being cross-trained and developed with greater scope, complexity and deepened organizational investment, it makes managing these employees more critical because they are being entrusted with even more proprietary knowledge and access to sensitive organizational information and relationships with stakeholders. Simply put, the organization is investing more in these employees, and the care and attention managers provide, or fail to provide, may impede or enhance such investment.

Third, there are both the wrong reasons and the right reasons that employees are transferred, and both play a role in how managers ultimately shape and direct these employees' behaviors. Some of the wrong reasons employees may be transferred include disagreements with a boss or co-workers in the previous department, something that may be a sign of future trouble. There may have been a poor fit with the prior job, something that will require the new manager to ensure that the employee has the proper knowledge/skills and attitude/motivation to perform in the new context. Some of the right reasons for transfers include a better fit with the interests/skills of the employee and the new job, something that signals to all employees a willingness on the part of the company to work with individuals on finding a good work situation. The ability to become cross-trained on new products, work processes, systems, etc., is another right reason for transferring an employee. This, too, signals to employees the organization's investment in, and commitment to, its workforce, and it places special consideration on the new manager to ensure that the organization continues to receive a fair return on that investment.

Finally, promoted employees, in particular, are often in a unique role to make or break broader employee engagement strategies. This is because these individuals may have been promoted from within, largely due to their technical, subject-matter or relationship expertise. Because many front-line supervisors and managers are largely responsible for meeting tactical goals, these newly promoted employees may emphasize production issues over people ones, thereby creating unintended tensions and consequences with employees. Conversely, a desire to be liked by employees — many of whom may have been former co-workers and friends — may cause a newly promoted employee to emphasize harmonious working relationships at the expense of tactical goals.

What We Know about *Transferred or Promoted Employees* and Engagement

In general, employees want to "move up, move over, or they'll move out." As expected, because the supervisor or manager has direct influence on the ability of employees to be promoted or transferred, there is a direct correlation between the promotional opportunities accorded employees, their perceptions of the relationship they have with supervisors and managers, and their engagement to the organization.

A review of data from the "2006-07 National Workforce Engagement Benchmark Study" indicates that these transferred or promoted employees appreciate these opportunities. (See "Correlation Between Promotion Rate and Supervisor Index Ratings" on page 76.) And not only does the Supervisor Index increase as the number of promotions increase, so does the engagement of the employee to his/her organization. (See "Correlation Between Promotions and Engagement" on page 76.)

Correlation Between Promotion Rate and Supervisor Index Ratings

Promotion Rate	Supervisor Index
Employees not promoted in the past three years	3.4
Employees promoted once in the past three years	3.7
Employees promoted twice in the past three years	3.9
Employees promoted three times in the past three years	4.0

Note: Based on a five-point scale, with 5 equaling "strongly agree" and 1 equaling "strongly disagree."

Advancement should never be given if an employee doesn't have the requisite skills, experiences, competencies and knowledge to perform meaningful work. Nonetheless, providing opportunities to qualified candidates has a dramatic impact on their desires to "work harder, stay longer and recommend the organization as a great place to work." Nearly 95 percent of employees promoted

Correlation Between Promotions and Engagement

According to the "2008-09 National Workforce Engagement Benchmark Study," 40 percent of all employees are fully engaged, 24 percent are reluctant and 36 percent are unengaged.

Number of Promotions	Engagement
No promotions	35% fully engaged
	24% reluctant
	41% unengaged
One promotion	47% fully engaged
	26% reluctant
	27% unengaged
Two promotions	53% fully engaged
	21% reluctant
	27% unengaged
Three-plus promotions	57% fully engaged
	25% reluctant
	18% unengaged

three times or more in the past three years have a good relationship with their supervisor, compared to three quarters (76 percent) of employees promoted once or twice, and 74 percent of employees not promoted at all.

Employees who agree their manager has explained the performance expectations of their job are significantly more likely to receive promotions than employees who disagree with the statement. Sixty-eight percent of employees who were not promoted agree with the statement, rising to 74 percent of those promoted once, 78 percent of those promoted twice and 92 percent of those promoted three times or more in the past three years.

Not surprisingly, employees who have been promoted in the past three years receive significantly more training programs/courses related to their job. Forty-five percent of employees who have been promoted at least once agree they regularly attend training programs, compared to 35 percent of those not promoted.

To keep the best, employers must be ready to move employees up or over, or employees will wind up moving out. Providing training and development and opportunities for advancement are investments that pay themselves back very quickly through better attitudes and behaviors from employees, and increased satisfaction and retention of customers.

Strategies to Engage *Transferred or Promoted Employees*

- Use similar selection criteria for internal transfers or promotions as is used with external hires.
- Determine the scope of the new role, and define clear performance expectations.
- Invest heavily in training and development for newly transferred and/or promoted employees.
- Identify the potential challenge of placing a superstar employee in a managerial role.
- Provide coaching and mentoring, especially for managerial roles.
- Recognize that once an employee is transferred or promoted, there is a tendency for the employee to want to be transferred or promoted again.

Use Similar Selection Criteria for Internal Transfers or Promotions as Is Used With External Hires

One benefit the organization achieves when transferring and promoting from within is the built-in knowledge the employer has about the employee's fit with the company, as well as the employee's track record and work style, among other characteristics. Regardless, when opportunities for movement or advancement arise, organizations should not minimize the importance of using similar selection criteria for internal transfers or promotions as it does for external hires. This is important for four reasons:

- Companies want to find the right person, for the right job, at the right time, and this necessarily means exploring all reasonable and potential options for qualified candidates in the talent management pipeline — including individuals from both within and outside the organization.
- Using similar selection criteria for both ensures consistency in hiring practices, providing the organization with the assurance that it has reached a decision through a fair and deliberate process.
- Such a move signals to employees that they are not automatically transferred or promoted simply because of their favored insider status. Rather, it heightens the awareness that the organization is interested in seeking the best qualified person for the job from all sources, and that can go a long way toward avoiding either an entitlement mentality on the part of the employee or perpetuating a paternalistic culture of employee dependence on the employer.
- Using similar criteria provides recently transferred or promoted individuals legitimacy in their new role by creating a situation in which the individual had to meet current competitive standards for opportunities elsewhere within the organization.

Determine the Scope of the New Role, and Define Clear Performance Expectations

As with any employee, defining, communicating and monitoring clear performance expectations is a managerial necessity. This becomes even more important for newly transferred or promoted employees because these individuals are taking on different duties and responsibilities in their new role. Often, however, managers simply — and incorrectly — assume that because an employee already has an affiliation with and understanding of the organization, he/she should inherently be aware of some of the unique aspects of the new job. Making explicit and intentional the scope of the new role, as well as setting clear performance expectations for transferred or promoted employees, is necessary if success in the new context is to be achieved.

This is especially challenging for promoted employees. Higher-level positions, even those just slightly above the position from which an employee was recently promoted, typically have broader and more complex measures of performance. There is a frequent tendency on the part of recently promoted employees, however, to be tempted to perform duties normally associated with the position from which the individual was promoted. While perhaps understandable — after all, the employee may have been promoted because of sound technical proficiency as an individual contributor — the scope of work required in higher-level positions should be markedly different from lower-level ones, and employees need to be aware of their new and emerging expectations. Training and development, among other interventions, is one way to ensure success for newly transferred and/or promoted employees.

Invest Heavily in Training and Development for Newly Transferred and/or Promoted Employees

Because the organization should be using similar selection criteria for transfers and promotions as it does for external hires, so too should similar training and development opportunities provided to external hires be afforded to internal individuals who take on new roles and responsibilities. Newly transferred and/or promoted employees often understand the broader organization's mission, context and issues; however, when it comes to the new performance expectations, internal employees likely need additional training on the work associated with their new role.

Many companies tend do to a much better job of training on business-specific and technical knowledge, and provide less emphasis given to so-called "soft skills" associated with management (people, process and communication skills). Ironically, it is the latter skill set that typically defines the nature and scope of most higher-level roles, and there tends to be the need for this type of training given that the sphere of influence is greater for supervisors and managers.

Training and development needs should necessarily flow from the performance expectations of the job, and should build upon and expand the existing knowledge, skills and abilities of the newly transferred or promoted individual. Managers are in the best position to work with the employee to assess training needs, and then provide the resources necessary for the acquisition of new knowledge and skills. Ensuring that internally transferred and promoted individuals have access to appropriate training and development for their new roles provides the organization with an ability to have performance expectations more rapidly met and a return on investment realized.

Identify the Potential Challenge of Placing a Superstar Employee in a Managerial Role

As noted, sometimes employees are promoted to a supervisor or managerial role on the basis of their technical competence or proficiency as an individual contributor.

Nowhere is this more evident than the frequent circumstance in many organizations of placing a superstar employee in a managerial role in either the same or different department. While obviously wanting to reward, invest in and capitalize on the energy, drive and expertise of a superstar employee, there are some potential challenges that managers need to be cognizant of when promoting superstars.

There often are two groups of people who are affected by such a move: the group that is losing the superstar employee and the group that the superstar employee is now managing. For the former group, colleagues (and the manager) are losing a valuable, effective member of the team who produced concrete and frequently above-average results. Even when other capable individuals exist to fulfill the role vacated by the superstar's advancement, there is often a lag or gap in productivity because "filling the superstar's shoes" often is a big task. The second group that is affected by a superstar promotion is the group of employees who will be working for the recently promoted employee. As discussed more fully in Chapter 5, superstars themselves operate in exceptional ways and often are a challenge to manage because of their ability to make decisions faster and expect results quicker. Thus, when placed in a management role, superstar employees often are tempted to superimpose their work style on other employees and to hold otherwise reasonably productive individuals to an artificially high standard. Like other recently promoted employees, superstars, too, are likely to fall into the tempting trap of wanting to do the work typically associated with the role from which they were recently promoted. They might feel it more expedient to do the work themselves rather than have an employee — who the superstar should now be managing — perform the job. Coaching and mentoring are one way that experienced managers and leaders can facilitate any employees' transition to an effective managerial role.

Provide Coaching and Mentoring, Especially for Managerial Roles

In addition to training and development, coaching and mentoring are widely used approaches to prepare employees for advancement opportunities. Coaching entails having a peer, manager or external source work with an employee to develop skills, provide reinforcement and offer feedback. Coaching can be very specific, used on an ad hoc basis (e.g., to assist a salesperson in improving closing techniques), or be an ongoing, long-term relationship (e.g., senior leaders who use outside coaches as a sounding board for problems).

Mentoring programs are formal relationships that typically are established and sanctioned by the organization. A mentor is an experienced employee who helps a less experienced employee through a long-term developmental relationship. The mentor assists the protégé by providing information about the organization, including the resources and opportunities available to the employee, often for the purpose of assisting the employee in career development matters. Both coaching and mentoring are interpersonal skill-building approaches that can augment other training and development approaches and can assist in providing a basis for opportunities for advancement.

Recognize That Once an Employee Is Transferred or Promoted, There Is a Tendency for the Employee to Want to Be Transferred or Promoted Again

Transfers and promotions are both exciting and potentially intimidating prospects for employees. However, once individuals are comfortable in their new roles and start to enjoy the success that comes with mastering new duties, responsibilities, knowledge and challenges, these transferred and promoted employees tend to deepen their confidence levels. As a result, once an employee is transferred or promoted, there is a tendency for the employee to want to be transferred or promoted again. Sometimes individuals assume they can take on more opportunities, and they may, in fact, be ready to do so. Often, however, employees who get comfortable in a new role and are desirous of added or different responsibilities may tend to forget the learning curve and frustrations they initially experienced. They may romanticize the ease and fluidity with which they acquired their now proficient capabilities. Obviously, organizations should handle subsequent transfers and promotions on a case-by-case basis driven, to a large extent, by company needs and the capacity of the individual employee to embrace a new and different role. In most organizations, advancement opportunities may become more limited the higher an individual progresses simply due to the lack of available or needed positions. Thus, consideration should be given to providing job enlargement, enrichment and rotation, as discussed in Chapter 3, for employees who have reasonably mastered their new role and are looking for greater challenges and opportunities.

Action Planning Log for Engaging *Transferred or Promoted Employees*

Employee Name	Specific Actions Planned to Engage Employee

What is the organization doing especially well to engage *Transferred or Promoted Employees*?

In what ways can the organization improve its efforts to engage *Transferred or Promoted Employees*?

chapter 8
ENGAGING LONG-TERM EMPLOYEES

Who Are *Long-Term Employees,* and Why Are They Important?

In the sped-up timeline that characterizes the new economy of the 21st century, long-term employees typically are those who are with an organization five to seven years or longer. Because the average employee tends to stay with an organization approximately four years, it seems ironic that "long term" could apply to someone who, chronologically, may still be quite young. To be fair, long-term is context-specific, and may vary dramatically based on industry, occupation and even length of tenure in a specific job.

Long-term employees are those who are viewed euphemistically as "friends and family" of the organization — those who have exhibited their loyalty to the organization by remaining employed while others may have moved on to other opportunities. As a result, these individuals represent the repository of intellectual and relationship capital in the organization, and are likely have deep knowledge of the organization and a long history with multiple stakeholders. For some organizations, long-term employees may even be the "face" of the company to its multiple publics.

From a management perspective, long-term employees pose tremendous opportunities and challenges. First, these individuals may be seen as de facto leaders and may command attention of important internal and external decision makers. Their views might be given greater weight because of tenure, and there may be a presumption that they are smarter or more in tune with the organization's needs. This could, of course, be problematic if information conveyed by these well-respected long-term employees is wrong, outdated or biased.

Second, the nature of rewarding and recognizing long-term employees is highly variable in many organizations. For some individuals, they will be highly compensated, due in some ways to the scope and impact of their role being relatively high in the organization chart. Others may have high salaries simply due to their length of service in the organization, regardless of position or accomplishments. Some long-term employees are, in fact, "rewarded" by being given less responsibility and/or being transferred around. These individuals may be well liked, but are viewed as ineffective, outdated, "hangers on" or retired on the job. Still other long-term employees may be highly functioning, capable, dynamic individuals who are the 20 percent of the employees who do 80 percent of the work.

Finally, some long-term employees represent those who are truly "trapped" in their jobs. These individuals are at a point in their careers in which they are comfortable with their job and the organization, the salary they command is decent, and they may find it difficult to replicate their internal work situation in the open labor market. In addition to trapped long-term employees, organizations also may cope with sidelined or marginalized individuals. In essence, these employees are problematic, but the organization is unwilling to fire them. Regrettably, the harm they can cause to the organization isn't marginalized or sidelined because their voice is still strong; they perceive their effectiveness to be more valued and necessary than it really is by others.

What We Know About *Long-Term Employees* and Engagement

According to the Bureau of Labor Statistics' "Tenure in 2006 Report," roughly 1-in-5 employees has been with his/her organization six to nine years, 1-in-10 has been with his/her company 10 to 14 years, and another 1-in-6 has been with his/her organization 15 years or more.

The levels of engagement for these tenured groups, as well as the drivers of engagement, vary widely. (See "Tenure and Engagement Levels.") For each of these tenured groups, "daily satisfaction" is the No. 1 driver of workforce engagement. Additional drivers of engagement for each of the tenured groups are as follows:

Six- to nine-year employees:
- Ethics, diversity and safety
- Reputation management

Tenure and Engagement Levels	
Tenure	Engagement Level
6-9 years	44% fully engaged
	25% reluctant
	32% unengaged
10-19 years	51% fully engaged
	16% reluctant
	33% unengaged
20-plus years	43% fully engaged
	15% reluctant
	42% unengaged
National Benchmark	43% fully engaged
	25% reluctant
	32% unengaged

- Stakeholder input.

10- to 19-year employees:

- Training and development
- Ethics, diversity and safety
- Reputation management.

20-plus-year employees:

- Reputation management
- Stakeholder input.

Ethics is a top-down, not bottom-up, process. Employees will look at their supervisors and managers to decide how to handle an ethical problem that may arise. If they believe their supervisors or managers would cut ethical corners to improve profit, the employees will act the same.

Employees with tenure of six to nine years have the weakest perceptions of the ethical fitness of their organization. While 63 percent of these employees believe their organization is highly ethical, 1-in-4 disagrees with this statement (24 percent). These scores are at parity with the perceptions of ethics of other tenured groups measured in the national benchmark study.

Some experts have argued the "golden rule" is all a supervisor needs to understand to manage employees. If this is the case, managers have some distance to go, especially with their more tenured employees. From the "2008-09 National Workforce Engagement Benchmark Study," employees with their organization more than six years are significantly less positive than less tenured employees. (See "Levels of Positivity Among Tenured and Less Tenured Employees" on page 87.)

Again, the more experience the employee has with his/her supervisor or manager, the more time he/she has to see if the boss "walks the talk," the more negative his/her perceptions of fairness and the weaker the impression of his/her boss.

Strategies to Engage *Long-Term Employees*

- Capture and share knowledge of long-term employees with others.
- Ensure these employees have meaningful work that positively affects their identities.
- Emphasize broader career and professional development aspects of organizational affiliation.
- Implement reward, recognition and development approaches that make sense.
- Use long-term employees as coaches/mentors for new and mid-career employees.

Capture and Share Knowledge of Long-Term Employees With Others

Although long-term employees are defined as those with five to seven years or longer in the organization, many people naturally gravitate toward thinking of long-term employees as those who are of a more advanced age. Indeed, one of the most pressing challenges facing many organizations today is the loss of intellectual capital through pending retirements. Even in settings in which the graying of the workforce isn't occurring as predominantly, there is a need to capture and share the organizationally relevant knowledge of long-term employees with others.

Simply put, employees represent the intellectual capital of an organization. The knowledge, relationships, experiences, successful practices and lessons learned from long-term employees needs to be codified in a more systemic manner if others in the organization are to analyze, understand and use this information for future purposes. Too often, however, such a treasure trove of talent is permitted to "walk out the door" without a full appreciation for the wealth of information that has been accumulated during years of work in an industry or organization. One aspect of knowledge management entails capturing relevant knowledge from long-term employees, and one way to do this is through a purposeful and intentional process of documenting and cataloguing the implicit or tacit information held by individual employees through formal interviews, observations and reflections, among other activities.

Whatever approaches organizations ultimately employ, the goal should be to identify the relevant knowledge that long-term employees have about key components of their jobs, the organization and the industry. One way to ensure

Levels of Positivity Among Tenured and Less Tenured Employees

	More than Six Years' Tenure	Less than Six Years' Tenure
People are treated with respect and appreciation	57% agree	64% agree
Differences among individuals are both respected and valued at this organization	55% agree	62% agree
Company policies are carried out in a fair and just manner	51% agree	59% agree
I believe this organization is highly ethical	62% agree	65% agree

long-term employees remain vital, contributing members of the organization also involves ensuring that these employees continue to perform meaningful work that positively affects their identities.

Ensure These Employees Have Meaningful Work That Positively Affects Their Identities

One clear advantage that organizations have in retaining long-term talent is the ability for employees to become deeply knowledgeable about the organization and its strengths and challenges. Another advantage for companies is the potential for these employees to be well-networked within and outside the company, including solid relationships with customers, business partners, industry/trade professionals and members of the community at-large. As long-term employees deepen their investment in and commitment to the organization, so too do they look for reciprocity of the relationship. This includes recognition of their loyalty and extends to the nature of work they perform for the company. Managers of long-term employees should work with these individuals — especially those who are solid, capable contributors — to determine the nature of work that best honors their experience while keeping them engaged in meaningful work.

Naturally, employees with greater experience and proven track records should be afforded courtesies, to the extent possible, in choosing schedules and exercising autonomy and discretion in performing work. Beyond this, managers might seek to assign long-term employees to special projects that capitalize on their knowledge or perspectives. In some instances, long-term employees might be best suited to leverage their spheres of influence outside the organization for new business development opportunities. In other cases, employees might best represent the company through community outreach endeavors. Exceptional and strategic long-term employees might even find a leadership role in community, trade or professional settings, thereby enhancing both the individual's and the organization's reputation.

Regardless of the nature, scope and impact of work, long-term employees should be respected and valued for their loyalty and, to the extent possible, be recognized with special considerations in the workplace that positively affect their personal and professional identities.

Emphasize Broader Career and Professional Development Aspects of Organizational Affiliation

Frequent turnover and a "what's in it for me now" philosophy tends to dominate most workplaces. With the average employee spending fewer than five years in an organization, most individuals have a job-specific focus to their work affili-ations. Long-term employees, however, provide companies with a reasonable degree of workforce stability, and likely have made contributions that extend beyond the job in which they originally were hired. Thus, instead of focusing on job-specific issues, employees should work with individuals to emphasize the broader career- and professional-development aspects of a lengthier affiliation with the organization.

As is the case for transferred and/or promoted employees, long-term employees need to know what their future potential looks like, in terms of opportunities for advance-ment, types of positions available, time-in-job requirements, and knowledge, skills, abilities and competencies needed for the future. Generally, this type of information should be provided by the employee's direct manager, although career development is, ultimately, the responsibility of the individual employee. In some instances, the career development discussion between a manager and long-term employee might center on whether the organization is still the place for the employee. Great care should be afforded these discussions, as the goal is not simply to devalue a long-term employee; rather, the goal is to have an honest assessment of whether the organization is continuing to meet the individual's needs, and whether the individual is continuing to make meaningful, reasonable contributions given the scope of his/her role and level of responsibility.

In any event, managers should try to engage long-term employees in a more intentional, deliberate and ongoing process to renew and enhance their knowl-edge, skills and experiences. Related to this, naturally, are reward, recognition and development approaches that make sense, given the long-term employees' situation and future plans.

Implement Reward, Recognition and Development Approaches That Make Sense

As discussed at the outset of this chapter, compensation systems for long-term employees are varied based on the level, nature and impact of work an employee performs. Therefore, this discussion centers less on issues related to pay, and instead focuses on the broad reward, recognition and development approaches that organizations should implement, given the characteristics of long-term employees. In general, reward practices for long-term employees should focus less on monetary aspects of work (while not outright ignoring them, either), and more on profes-sional development, quality of work, recognition, opportunities to improve skills and expand work-related interests, and work-life balance issues.

Employees who anticipate maintaining their status as an individual-contributor employee should be expected and required to maintain technical currency and proficiency in their work, and managers should ensure that these employees receive ongoing training for those purposes. For long-term employees who are making contributions in more strategic ways, providing access to development opportunities within and outside the organization are necessary. Customized development such as mentoring, participation in an advanced leadership development program, professional-development sabbaticals, assignments with community groups or other organizations, and special projects are all ways to deepen engagement and expand on the capacity of intellectual growth and development of high-potential long-term employees. Rewards should be provided to long-term employees at any level for their enhanced acquisition and application of new knowledge and skills that continue to make meaningful impact on their work performance. Managers are in the best position to encourage, monitor and make reward, recognition and development decisions for long-term employees, and such decisions will necessarily be customizable based on the intentions, expectations and demonstration of continued commitment to the organization by these individuals.

Use Long-Term Employees as Coaches/Mentors for New and Mid-Career Employees

Not surprisingly, long-term employees naturally are in the best position to help share knowledge, develop organizational capacity, and deepen the engagement of both themselves and other employees. Thus, certain long term employees should be used as coaches or mentors for new and mid-career employees. In determining which long-term employees should be coaches/mentors, managers must consider several factors.

First, the prospective coach/mentor should have sufficient technical knowledge and experience within the organization to be able to provide new and mid-career employees with accurate, relevant and current information about mission-centric information on key products, services and core knowledge. Second, the prospective coach/mentor should have sufficient depth and breadth of understanding about the organization's history, culture, future directions and intangible factors (e.g., informal relationships and networks) to be able to provide new and mid-career employees with useful perspectives about the politics and priorities of organizational life. Third, prospective coaches/mentors should have the right personal disposition and a willingness to share openly with junior colleagues their own feelings, lessons learned, pitfalls and other experiences that have shaped their experience in the company. Finally, the prospective coach/mentor should be appropriately recognized for the time, energy and effort such a role entails. This could range from providing formal or informal rewards and recognition for serving as a coach/mentor to allowing release time from other duties and responsibilities to engage in this important task.

Action Planning Log for Engaging *Long-Term Employees*

Employee Name	Specific Actions Planned to Engage Employee

What is the organization doing especially well to engage *Long-Term Employees*?

In what ways can the organization improve its efforts to engage *Long-Term Employees*?

chapter 9
ENGAGING TEMPORARY EMPLOYEES

Who Are *Temporary Employees,* and Why Are They Important?

As more organizations outsource and automate work and increasingly concentrate on core competencies associated with the company's mission, the need for robust workforces has declined. Indeed, in recent years many organizations have attempted to stabilize their workforces by making judicious hiring decisions concerning adding full-time, year-round employees. The result has been, in part, a greater reliance on temporary workers: those employees hired for a fixed duration to accomplish a specific purpose.

For the purposes of this book, temporary employees are defined to include seasonal employees, such as department store holiday employees. Contingent employees, or individuals hired for a specific purpose and/or project, are another example of temporary employees. Typically, seasonal and contingent employees are, indeed, employees of the organization; thus, they rely on the organization to pay their salaries, handle tax withholdings, provide any relevant benefits, set their work schedules, provide work-related tools and technology, and operate as an employer in good faith.

Independent contractors differ from other types of temporary employees because, by the virtue of their title as an "independent" contractor, they are not considered employees. The U.S. Internal Revenue Service provides guidance on clarifying whether someone is an employee or independent contractor.

In general, individuals likely will be considered employees if they receive "extensive" instruction on: (1) how, when or where to do the work they will perform; (2) what tools or equipment to use; and (3) where to purchase supplies and services. Individuals likely will be considered employees if they receive training about required procedures and methods.

Conversely, individuals likely will be considered independent contractors if they: (1) make significant investment in their work; (2) do not get directly reimbursed for expenses; (3) have the ability to make profit or loss on their work; and (4) receive no benefits from the company, such as health insurance and paid vacation. Readers are directed to www.irs.gov for further information on the differentiation between independent-contractor and employee status.

While there are legal and financial differences between independent contractors and employees, independent contractors may be similar to other forms of temporary employees from a management perspective: They perform work that is necessary for the organization's functioning, and may interact with customers, employees and other stakeholders. Thus, while managers may not have as much control over independent contractors as they do other types of temporary employees, recognizing the unique circumstances under which both independent contractors and temporary employees work is an important managerial imperative.

Temporary workers, by design, are hired to fill short-term needs of "production" problems. In doing so, these individuals may have similar responsibilities as existing employees, thereby requiring similar approaches used with traditional employees. There are a couple of additional areas of distinction that differentiate the dynamic between the manager and temporary employee. First, the "duality of loyalty" experienced by temporary employees who are employed by a staffing firm, yet work in a client organizational context, poses a challenge. Employees in this situation technically are employed by a staffing firm and may be considered distance-based employees by the staffing firm's management (see Chapter 10 for more on engaging distance-based employees). Managers, employees and customers at the client site may be the individuals with whom this type of employee has the most frequent interaction and affiliation, yet his/her loyalty as an employee tends to lie with the firm providing the employment opportunity.

Second, sometimes temporary employees — whether hired as seasonal help or through a staffing firm — act as "wannabe" employees of the organization in which they are performing work. In this situation, these employees desire a more permanent affiliation with the organization, and may work to curry favor with managers and employees in the hopes of one day joining the organization as a traditional employee. For some organizations, this arrangement is a natural evolution of the relationship between seasonal and/or temporary employees. Other organizations might restrict the ability of these employees to become more permanent members of the company, largely due to fiscal or operational realities that might constrain such a practice. Regardless, managers should be mindful that these "wannabe" employees likely desire a longer-term engagement with the organization, and should work to provide a welcoming environment that sets realistic boundaries and expectations.

What We Know About *Temporary Employees and Engagement*

According to the December 2007 Bureau of Labor Statistics employment report, nearly 2.5 million people are working in "temporary help services." Although not considered "employees" by the organization that uses them, these workers still are expected to work as smart and as hard on behalf of the customers as regular employees.

As described earlier in this chapter, however, there are legal implications to what a company can and cannot do with these employees in terms of increasing their engagement (and improving their behavior). In addition, companies will not provide training and development beyond what is required for the job. They will not promote or advance the temporary worker, primarily because it is not why the employee was hired. They will not go out of their way to provide work-life balance, which is the responsibility of the temporary agency.

As discussed earlier in this chapter, areas that are critical to the engagement and the desire of these temporary workers to work hard on behalf of customers are:

- Daily satisfaction
- Workforce selection
- Organizational orientation
- Tools and technology.

In the area of orientation and organizational onboarding, today's employees are generally satisfied with the performance of their supervisors and managers. In fact, it is one of the few areas considered a strength in the "2008-09 National Workforce Engagement Benchmark Study," although it is still below 2004-05 levels. Seven-in-ten of today's employees agree:

- They have a clear understanding of the company's mission, vision, values and objectives and the role they play in them (72 percent in 2008-09, down from 75 percent in 2004-05).
- The importance of ethical business conduct has been communicated to the employee throughout his/her employment (69 percent in 2008-09, down from 73 percent in 2004 05).
- The requirements and responsibilities of the job are well-defined (73 percent in 2008-09, up from 71 percent in 2004-05).
- The employee's manager has explained the performance expectations of the job (69 percent in 2008-09, down from 71 percent in 2004-05).

Employees are less positive about the tools and technology they are provided. It also seems reasonable to believe that a company's permanent employees would receive the most up-to-date tools and technology to perform at their maximum level, meaning that the perceptions of temporary workers may in fact be lower than the national benchmark results. "Tools and technology" is an area that individual employees believe is the responsibility of their direct supervisors, so the perceptions employees have about tools and technology directly affects their feelings about their boss. Consider:

- Seven-in-ten employees (73 percent) agree they "have the materials and equipment I need to do the job."

- Seven-in-ten employees (73 percent) agree they are given "enough authority to get my job done."
- Seven-in-ten employees (69 percent) believe "the tools and technology provided by the company are straightforward and easy to use."

However, the picture is less rosy when it comes to other issues related to tools and technology:

- Six-in-ten employees (63 percent) agree they "have control over the resources I use to do my work."
- Slightly more than half of employees (53 percent) are "encouraged to try new ways of doing things at work," while 1-in-5 employees (20 percent) are not.

In terms of "workforce selection," 69 percent of today's employees agree "the duties and responsibilities of my job were accurately explained to me during the interview process," a significant improvement from 2004-05 and 2006-07 levels. Why is this a concern? Temporary workers typically don't go through an interview process with the company they will work for, so the ability to explain the job duties and responsibilities falls to the supervisor and manager they will work for.

We already know that just 6-in-10 employees believe their supervisor "gives clearly defined performance goals and objectives," while nearly 1-in-5 (18 percent) disagrees. Worse yet, there has been no improvement in these scores in the past five years.

What is the clear implication for engaging temporary workers? If companies want to get the most out of their temps, they have to make the effort. Provide them an understanding of how they fit into the organization, even as a "nonemployee." Make the job challenging. Ensure there is a good fit between the skills/interests of the worker and the job. Provide adequate tools and technology that facilitate getting the job done. Temporary workers make a permanent impression on customers; therefore, managing their engagement is critical to company success.

Strategies to Engage *Temporary Employees*

- Recognize the role that temporary employees play in meeting organizational needs.
- Identify the scope of work, set appropriate boundaries and manage expectations accordingly.
- Provide necessary training, tools and technology for work performance.
- Effectively manage feedback and performance management processes.
- Treat temporary employees with common courtesy, dignity and respect.

Recognize the Role That Temporary Employees Play in Meeting Organizational Needs

As noted, there are several strategic, fiscal and operational necessities requiring the use of temporary employees in organizational settings. Managers who work with temporary employees should be able to identify, articulate and explain the business reasons for using this type of talent. The ability to communicate this understanding is important to several stakeholder groups. For example, traditional employees, or those who work on a more permanent, fixed basis for the organization, likely will wonder why the organization is not adding additional full-time staff. These employees also may view the use of temporary employees as a first step toward organizational restructuring, downsizing or discontinuation of work. Thus, it is necessary for managers to be clear and candid (to the extent they are able) about the business reasons for securing temporary talent.

In some cases, customers, business partners, vendors, suppliers and others might interface with temporary employees. Often, these stakeholders may not differentiate between whether someone they interact with is a traditional or temporary employee — and this may be intentional on the organization's part. The extent to which external stakeholders need to be aware of a status differentiation on the part of individual employees is, of course, context-specific and likely based on a need-to-know basis. Managers should use judgment and discretion in determining whether to release this information to individuals outside the organization and, when doing so, should exercise caution with respect to the personal and proprietary information that is disclosed.

Identify the Scope of Work, Set Appropriate Boundaries and Manage Expectations Accordingly

Like any employee over whom managers have responsibility for performance, temporary employees must have performance expectations identified, communicated and monitored. The nature of the temporary employee's assignment with an organization likely will dictate by whom and when issues, such as work scope and performance expectations, are communicated. In the case of independent contractors or temporary workers from a staffing/temporary agency, the nature of the work assignment might be outlined in an upfront contractual arrangement. In other cases, such as with seasonal or temporary project employees who are actually employed by the organization, the hiring manager or equivalent direct supervisor may outline and communicate such information. The unique circumstances under which temporary employees work — that is, the fixed-term duration that characterizes the nature of such work assignments — requires that managers exercise additional care with these employees. Setting appropriate boundaries could range from the type of access temporary workers have to organizational resources, to limiting the nature of work performed by the employee due to contractual or proprietary considerations. Managing expectations requires managers to act deftly to not falsely raise hopes of continued, long-term employment prospects, especially when it is impractical, impossible or improbable that such a prospect exists. While temporary employees bring some unique managerial considerations, they also have pragmatic needs, too, especially in areas related to training, tools and technology for work performance.

Provide Necessary Training, Tools and Technology for Work Performance

Clearly, the scope and nature of work to be performed by a temporary employee, coupled with the anticipated duration of the work assignment, are two variables that managers must consider when determining the type of training, tools and technology to provide. At the very least, training on basic operations, work flow and organization-specific practices — even if such training occurs informally or on the job — should be part of a temporary employee's orientation.

To maximize the effective contributions that temporary employees can make during their time in the organization, managers should allocate the appropriate job-specific tools and technology for the individual. Often, the tools and technology used in performing the work will be obvious, based on the inputs, throughputs and outputs of the job. Other times, an analysis of the job, including the expected outcomes and processes used to perform those outcomes, will yield information on the tools and technology needed. This is especially true with ad hoc projects for which the organization has little prior experience in orchestrating, and for whom temporary employees are being used to accomplish project-related tasks. The main managerial objective, therefore, is to determine when, how, by whom and under what conditions the provision of training, tools and technology for temporary workers must be arranged.

Effectively Manage Feedback and Performance Management Processes

Employees who perform any type of work value feedback on the nature of their job performance. Savvy managers realize that the sooner feedback is given in relationship to the occurrence of performance, the more likely that feedback will yield improved performance. While this model or approach works well in managing traditional employees, there are some nuances that managers must consider when giving feedback and managing the performance of temporary employees.

Employee motivation to perform is like a function of the individual's own work ethic and value system and is related to his/her time horizon and how he/she views affiliation with the job. In the case of employees who work for temporary/staffing agencies, for example, do the employees view their primary performance obligation to the place where work is performed or to the organization for which they are an employee? In this case, feedback on performance likely is informally given by the on-site manager to the individual employee, but formally given to the staffing/temporary agency which, in turn, gives formal performance management to the employee. Thus, navigating the potentially cumbersome and prickly politics of providing feedback and managing employee performance — especially with those workers who are not employees of the on-site manager — is, indeed, challenging. Proactively outlining and agreeing on how such processes should occur, as well as making all parties aware of the feedback and performance management protocol, is advisable. Finally, a large measure of common sense on the part of the manager and temporary employee, coupled with treating each other with common courtesy, dignity and respect, can go a long way toward enhancing relationships under these unique work arrangements.

Treat Temporary Employees With Common Courtesy, Dignity and Respect

Managers should recognize that daily satisfaction, selection, orientation, and tools and technology are key drivers of engagement for temporary employees. Because these presumably are some of the only organizationally sanctioned interventions managers can control with temporary employees, it is vital that these areas are addressed early and often. In addition to these practices, it is incumbent on managers to treat temporary employees with common courtesy, dignity and respect. To be fair, the attitudes that temporary employees (and, for that matter, managers and traditional employees) bring to the workplace will go a long way toward facilitating positive interactions between the temporary employee and organizational insiders.

There might be little in terms of tangible rewards managers can provide to temporary employees, given contractual, fiscal and other constraints. Therefore, it is necessary for managers to create a welcoming environment where temporary employees feel valued for their contributions — no matter how large or small, for whatever length of time. By doing so, managers send a signal to both temporary and traditional employees that the organization treats all individuals with dignity and respect and that, regardless of status, managers will lead by example and encourage others to do likewise. This should yield positive performance that takes place in a more pleasant workplace.

Action Planning Log for Engaging *Temporary Employees*

Employee Name	Specific Actions Planned to Engage Employee

What is the organization doing especially well to engage *Temporary Employees*?

In what ways can the organization improve its efforts to engage *Temporary Employees*?

chapter 10
ENGAGING DISTANCE-BASED EMPLOYEES

Who Are *Distance-Based Employees,* and Why Are They Important?

In a globally oriented, technologically-wired and interdependent world, the nature of work itself is more dynamic than ever. Organizational structures, systems and jobs themselves have evolved and adapted to this new world of work and, as a result, many companies are now comprised of distance-based workers. For the purposes of this book, distance-based work is characterized on both the type of employee and the degree of distance.

The following are representative of the types of employees referred to as distance-based workers:

- Geographically dispersed employees are those individuals who work in locations that are physically spread out from each other (e.g., a salesforce that is deployed into various markets around the United States to forge closer, field-based relationships with customers).
- Telecommuting employees are another type of distance-based employee. These are individuals who work from a remote location and connect to work, colleagues, business partners and/or customers through the telephone or other electronic means.
- Satellite office workers also are distance-based because the work of the satellite office is removed from that of the headquarters location.
- Mobile workers spend the bulk of their work time "in the field" at either organizational or client sites.
- Home-based workers are employees of an organization, but work nearly exclusively from their home offices.

While not all encompassing of every distance-based employment arrangement, these examples provide a backdrop to the definition of distance-based employees.

The degree of distance also is an important distinction when considering the management implications for distance-based work. For the purposes here, we delineate distance-based work as minimally, moderately or highly distant. Minimally distant work encompasses employees who seldom work in a remote location, such as working from a home or client site once or twice per month.

From a management perspective, no special, ongoing intervention is needed beyond the typical communication of performance expectations.

Moderately and highly distant work involves employees who regularly work without management supervision, and for whom the primary manager of the employee is located in a venue elsewhere from where the work is performed. For employees, moderately distant work likely involves a fairly equivalent mix of time spent working both in close proximity with their boss and at a distance; highly distant work is organized in such a way that the employee works highly independent of geographic proximity to his/her boss.

One aspect of the unique nature of distance-based work also involves managers who may supervise traditional employees, but for whom they, as managers, are considered distance-based employees. For example, only the branch manager of a satellite bank office who reports to his/her boss in another location may be considered a distance-based employee. All of the rest of the employees in that branch who report to that branch manager are not distance-based employees. Therefore, special consideration needs to be given to that branch manager based on the distance of the reporting relationship.

The management and engagement needs of distance-based employees, therefore, are important, often due to some perceptions and misconceptions about distance-based work. In some instances, senior leaders and managers may perceive that it is harder to manage distance-based employees in spite of advanced communication and electronic tools. There may be the misconception that distance-based employees are less explicitly committed to the organization. Managers also may view distance-based employees as potentially underperforming or too independent, while distance-based employees may feel isolated, disconnected or neglected by the larger organization.

What We Know About *Distance-Based Employees* and Engagement

The premise of this book is the importance of the relationship between an individual employee and his/her supervisor, and the impact this relationship has on the engagement of the employee and his/her subsequent behaviors. Perhaps no situation is more difficult than managing distance-based employees. As discussed, the inability to easily interact with the direct report (and vice versa) makes the relationship more difficult to build and sustain. Relying solely on communicating via e-mail is fraught with difficulties; we all have misinterpreted text, underlines or exclamation points. E-mails lack the personal touch so important to many relationships, and therefore can exacerbate an already difficult situation.

Communication is the key to maintaining positive relationships with distance-based employees. Many of these employees are supervisors or managers who work in satellite or branch offices (like a bank-branch manager or a retail store manager in a mall), so this section concentrates on the feelings of supervisors and managers from the "2008-09 National Workforce Engagement Benchmark Study." Unlike 2006-07, there are only two key drivers of engagement in 2008-09 for supervisors:

• Daily satisfaction
• Stakeholder input.

There was a significant shift in the levels of supervisor engagement. In fact, for the first time, supervisors are less fully engaged and more reluctant than individual contributors. In terms of engagement levels, 36 percent of supervisors are fully engaged, 30 percent are reluctant and 34 percent are unengaged — all significantly worse results than in 2006 (52 percent fully engaged, 16 percent reluctant and 31 percent unengaged). The low level of fully engaged supervisory employees, nearly the lowest of any demographic group, is of real concern. These are the employees who are asked to do more with less ... to improve daily processes through "better, cheaper, faster." These scores alone show the importance of targeting supervisors for additional training, development and attention. With regard to communication:

• Less than 6-in-10 supervisors (55 percent) agree that "the organization encourages open, honest communication," while nearly 1-in-4 supervisors disagrees (22 percent.)
• Nearly 6 in 10 supervisors (57 percent) agree "the organization regularly seeks input from employees to improve business practices, products and services," lower ratings than executives and middle management, and at parity with individual contributors.
• Less than half of all supervisors (48 percent) agree "an effort is made to get my input when decisions are made that impact me."
• Just 6-in-10 of all supervisors (66 percent) believe the company "provides me the information I need to make good decisions," while 1-in-6 disagrees (16 percent).
• Two-thirds of all supervisors (66 percent) believe "ethical issues are communicated throughout my employment," while 1-in-7 disagrees (14 percent).

Supervisors, even those who are distance-based, want advancement opportunities, whether in their same location, another branch or satellite office, or back at corporate. The 2008-09 national benchmark data shows that organizations weakened considerably since 2006-07. Consider:

- Less than 7-in-10 supervisors feel positively "the company considers internal employees for promotions and advancement (68 percent), down from 74 percent in 2006-07.
- Less than 6-in-10 supervisors (58 percent) feel their "performance on the job is judged fairly," down from 68 percent in 2006-07.
- Slightly more than half feel "qualified employees are usually allowed to transfer to better jobs" (54 percent), down from 64 percent in 2006-07.
- Slightly more than half (53 percent) believe the organization "provides opportunities for advancement," down from 58 percent in 2006-07.
- Less than half believe they have "opportunities for promotion within my department or division" (45 percent), down from 50 percent in 2006-07.
- Only 4-in-10 believe the company "does a good job of supporting employee career development" (41 percent), down from 48 percent in 2006-07.

Strategies to Engage *Distance-Based Employees*

- Determine the scope, nature and impact of distance-based employees on the organization.
- Identify changes to management styles and approaches that must occur.
- Allocate necessary tools and technology to manage employees.
- Develop communication strategies and provide specific opportunities to keep distance-based employees connected to the organization.
- Evaluate the effectiveness of work arrangements and make ongoing enhancements and improvements.

Determine the Scope, Nature and Impact of Distance-Based Employees on the Organization

As noted at the beginning of this chapter, both the type of employee and degree of distance frame how distance-based work affects the employee and his/her work. Thus, from a managerial perspective, one of the first tasks necessary is to determine the scope, nature and impact of distance-based employees on the organization. Managers must consider whether distance-based work is an integral, widespread component of the organization's culture and operations, or if distance-based work is highly situational and relegated to context-specific jobs and people. If it is the former, the organization likely has policies, resources and approaches already in place to manage some aspects of distance-based work. In cases in which distance-based work is the exception to the rule, however, there likely exist fewer formal systems to handle this dynamic. When this occurs, managers and employees typically are the ones who have to work together to develop solutions to the inherent differences and needs resulting from distance-based work. One obvious requirement for managers, therefore, is the ongoing need to identify changes to management styles and approaches that must occur when employees engage in any form of distance-based work.

Identify Changes to Management Styles and Approaches That Must Occur

Thoughtful managers reflect on the effectiveness of their work, incorporating feedback from employees and others, as well as their own critical analysis of their strengths and weaknesses, and use this information for improved future management practice and performance. Nowhere is such thoughtful reflection and action on the manager's part more appreciated than when it comes to managing people, processes and circumstances that are unique and alter the management dynamic between superior and subordinate. Managing distance-based employees is one such dynamic.

After identifying the scope, nature and impact distance-based employees have on the organization, one natural evolution for managers is considering the need to potentially change management styles and approaches to managing distance-based employees. While the type of work, the characteristics of employees and the manager, and the employee and organization's track record with distance-based work all are important ingredients, several additional managerial changes need to be considered. Even though none of these styles and approaches are unique to distance-based work, the need for thoughtful reflection and action is more paramount given the nature of distance-based work and employees.

Distance-based work necessarily requires a certain level of trust managers have in their employees. Management styles can range from the autocratic/dictatorial style, in which managers tend to make unilateral decisions and inform employees of those decisions, to the permissive/consultative style, in which managers tend to seek input from employees and involve them early and often in decision-making. Related to management style is a decision-making continuum ranging from highly centralized to highly decentralized approaches. Without being overprescriptive, the nature of distance-based work necessarily will require managers to operate using the permissive/consultative management style and decentralized decision-making approach — perhaps with more frequency than would typically be the case. This is largely due to the logistics involved in managing from a distance, where command-and-control oversight — which is easier to achieve when employees work in close physical proximity to their boss — is somewhat impractical. Finally, managers also must work to ensure that distance-based employees have allocated to them the tools, technology and other interventions to manage employees who are distance-based.

Allocate Necessary Tools and Technology to Manage Employees

Allocation of tools and technology includes providing the materials regularly needed for employees to be effective working on site or off site. Distance jobs often require employees to use specific hardware, interact with specific software and have access to specialized databases or data sets in order to research issues, solve problems and accomplish tasks remotely. These employees need to not only have access, but also an understanding of how the tools and technology are to be used in performing work, and the ability to request additional tools and technology to enhance overall work processes and productivity. The manager bears responsibility for identifying, locating, sourcing, allocating and maintaining tools and technology for an employee to use at distance locations. When inevitable equipment breakdowns occur, repairs should occur quickly and, when feasible, temporary replacements should be made available. Finally, distance-based employees need to understand the financial resources available to them based on their unique working situation, including any limitations that preclude the ability to secure tools and technology for performing work. Budgetary responsibility, purchasing power, spending authority and reimbursable items all are issues that need to be identified, clarified, communicated and reinforced to employees on a regular basis.

Develop Communication Strategies and Provide Specific Opportunities to Keep Distance-Based Employees Connected to the Organization

While effective communication between managers and employees is the hallmark of any productive, positive working relationship, the nature of distance-based work requires intentional communication that goes above and beyond the traditional office-based strategies. Especially important for moderately or highly distant employees, the ability to be in regular contact with their manager, peers and others is important to keeping these employees engaged. Thus, managers must ensure that meeting logistics, even those facilitated by electronic means, occur frequently and with proper coordination — something that may pose an additional level of complexity when team-oriented, distance-based employees cross multiple time zones. Managers also should arrange appropriate "come back to home" opportunities in which distance-based employees have a physical place to perform work in the "headquarters" (broadly defined) location. These events also go a long way toward building the psychosocial connections employees have with their organization, and can provide a reasonable degree of connectedness when planned and arranged effectively. Finally, having a cadre of distance-based workers in a manager's portfolio of talent may dictate that the manager be proactive in "managing by driving or flying around" — literally going to locations in which employees perform their work. This is done to enhance communication, build rapport, maintain oversight of work and, in general, signal to the distance-based employees that the organization is willing to come to them, too, in addition to placing a share of the burden on these employees to manage their own linkages to the company's site-based locations.

Evaluate the Effectiveness of Work Arrangements and Make Ongoing Enhancements and Improvements

Clearly, the nature of distance-based work, and the managerial interventions and employee responsibilities inherent in these varied arrangements, requires ongoing efforts to seek input from affected stakeholders and make enhancements and improvements. The benefits of permitting distance-based employees to accomplish all or a portion of their work remotely must outweigh the real and perceived costs of making this opportunity available. As noted in Chapter 6 during a related discussion concerning returning employees, regularly evaluating the effectiveness of providing distance options and opportunities to remote employees needs to occur. This requires managers to work with others (e.g., HR) to track the return on investment the organization achieves in permitting talent to work from a distance.

One measure of success, obviously, is the retention, satisfaction and engagement exhibited by distance-based employees, and this information can be gleaned from both formal means (e.g., surveying a sufficient number of distance-based employees) and informal methods (e.g., frequent interaction and communication between the manager and the distance-based employee). As distance-based work continues to evolve and emerge, ongoing attention to the strategic, fiscal, technological and practical considerations of this staffing approach needs to occur.

Action Planning Log for Engaging *Distance-Based Employees*

Employee Name	Specific Actions Planned to Engage Employee

What is the organization doing especially well to engage *Distance-Based Employees*?

In what ways can the organization improve its efforts to engage *Distance-Based Employees*?

chapter 11
ENGAGING EMPLOYEES WITH SPECIAL NEEDS OR CIRCUMSTANCES

Who Are *Employees with Special Needs or Circumstances,* and Why Are They Important?

While tempting to classify employees with special needs or circumstances as simply a disability-related label, the reality of modern organizational life is that nearly all employees will, at some point in their working careers, be an employee that has a special need or circumstance requiring managerial intervention — be it disability-related or otherwise. In this context, employees with special needs or circumstances refers to an entire spectrum of issues: employees who are physically and/or mentally challenged; those who are part of dual-career couples; employees who work and attend school either full time, part time or both; and individuals with family obligations that might include child care, elder care or some other form of care for a loved one — in some cases providing care to more than one individual simultaneously. While not exhaustive, this framework provides a representative backdrop to the types of special needs and circumstances confronting employees in nearly every organization today.

With the advent of the Americans with Disabilities Act of 1990 (ADA) and the Family and Medical Leave Act of 1993 (FMLA), among other public policies at the federal, state and local levels, many organizations are becoming more responsive to, and mindful of, the diversity of experiences, circumstances and perspectives of their workforces. In general, companies are likely to do a good job of providing reasonable accommodations for physically and mentally challenged employees, especially in light of the aforementioned legal encouragements for such compliance. In recent years, however, an expanded definition of special needs and circumstances has emerged. Organizations now more fully and openly reflect the sociocultural and personal-demographic characteristics of the labor markets in which businesses operate, and this has yielded an emphasis on work-life effectiveness initiatives in several settings. There are, however, special considerations and acknowledgements that must be identified when referring to employees with special needs and circumstances.

To be sure, employees with special needs and circumstances are the diversity of the workplace personified. The illumination of the human condition in the workplace has brought more widespread attention to issues that once were relegated to the side-lines or ignored outright. Advocates for the disabled, working parents, the mentally challenged and those providing care to loved ones, among many other groups, all have helped enlighten corporate leaders to change, develop or enhance organizational policies and practices to be more inclusive of the realities facing today's employees. Thus, the fact that savvy organizations now pay attention to these matters signals the impact such advocacy and enlightenment is having in the workplace.

While most cutting-edge organizations are responding to the diversity of issues faced by employees with special needs and circumstances, they are doing so with the explicit, concurrent realization that employees are expected to perform and make meaningful, ongoing contributions to the organization's broader efforts. Simply put, organizations and those who lead and manage them are not an employee's parent, religious leader, psychologist, counselor or social worker. Instead, they are responsible to multiple stakeholders for fulfilling a stated mission in an efficient and effective manner. The organization can fulfill its mission while simultaneously signaling organizational commitment to its employees. Organizations can serve employees with special needs and circum-stances quite effectively, and do so on a sustainable basis when these same employees (and others) commit to performing to the best of their abilities.

What We Know About *Employees with Special Needs or Circumstances* and Engagement

As described in this book, the definition of special needs and circumstances has expanded in the past few decades from one of physical limitations to one that is inclu-sive of work-family issues. In most cases, the accommodation of physical limitations has been dealt with, providing opportunities for these special-needs employees.

The Department of Defense, for example, established the Computer/Electronic Accommodations Program (CAP) to eliminate employment barriers for employees with disabilities. CAP provides accommodations to individuals who are blind, have low vision, are deaf, are hard of hearing or have a dexterity, communication, cognitive or learning disability.

Other companies have provided interpreters, readers or other personal assistance, modified job duties, restructured work sites, provided flexible work schedules or work sites, or obtained accessible technology or other workplace adaptive equipment. However, companies (and supervisors) are now dealing with the difficult issues related to work-life balance.

Supervisors often are caught in a valley of ambiguity, trying to maneuver between one mountaintop of policy requirements and another mountaintop of flexible, customizable approaches that permit supervisors to do the right thing for employees. In terms of work-life balance, three groups are highlighted in the "2008-09 National Workforce Engagement Benchmark Study":

- Households with children
- Households caring for a loved one other than a child
- Households caring for both children and an adult loved one (what many refer to as the "Sandwich Generation").

In most cases, there was little difference in work-life balance issues between households with children and households without:

- Sixty percent of employees in households with children agreed that their manager recognizes the importance of personal and family life, compared with 60 percent of employees in households without children.
- Fifty-five percent of employees in households with children believed their company provides family friendly benefits, while 52 percent of households without children believe the same.
- Fifty-one percent of employees in households with children agreed "this company is sensitive to the needs of employees," compared to 49 percent of employees in households without children, a significant improvement from 2006 levels.

The story is somewhat different when reviewing households taking care of an adult loved one:

- Fifty-four percent of employees in households taking care of an adult loved one agreed that managers recognize the importance of personal and family life, compared to 61 percent of employees in households without an adult being cared for.
- Forty-five percent of employees in households taking care of an adult agreed that the company is sensitive to the needs of employees, compared to 51 percent of employees in households without an adult being cared for.

Today's supervisors and managers need to learn and adopt new strategies to assist employees struggling in the Sandwich Generation. Although the ratings are more positive than in 2006-07, pressure will continue to build on employers to assist these hard-pressed employees, now numbering more than 20 million. (See "Responses from the Sandwich Generation" on page 118.)

Strategies to Engage *Employees with Special Needs or Circumstances*

- Recognize that employees appreciate managers who are concerned about their holistic well-being.
- Identify employees who face special needs or circumstances.
- Operate with fairness and discretion when handling sensitive employee matters.
- Provide flexible work arrangements, as feasible.
- Develop specific interventions to address employee needs.
- Assess, clarify and prioritize approaches to engage employees with special needs or circumstances.

Recognize That Employees Appreciate Managers Who Are Concerned About Their Holistic Well-Being

First and foremost, managers must realize that employees have a life beyond the workplace. How a manager responds to the balancing act employees face in dealing with their personal and professional lives sends a signal about the organization's and manager's commitment to individual, holistic well-being. To achieve this, however, managers must have organizational support (starting at the top, with senior leaders). And, the resources that will help managers and employees should be explicitly communicated to the workforce. This also means that when an employee feels stressed and/or overwhelmed due to personal issues, managers should attempt to act, whenever possible, by adjusting work schedules, making referrals to counselors, listening to employees and, in general, providing reasonable assistance within the boundaries of employer-employee relationships. Of course, managers must learn to recognize the differences between an isolated incident (something that happens to an employee on a rare basis) and a pattern of behavior (something that may signal a lack of discipline and life management on the part of employees). As a result, managers should respond accordingly and be mindful that accommodations should be made to employees who have been identified as facing special needs or circumstances.

Identify Employees Who Face Special Needs or Circumstances

Employees who face special needs or circumstances, and for whom managerial or organizational intervention is necessary, need to be identified. This identification can be initiated in several ways. Employee-initiated disclosure of special needs or circumstances occurs when individuals alert their managers (or HR, or both) of their need for assistance. Managers who are actively involved in interacting with

Responses from the Sandwich Generation

	Households Currently in the Sandwich Generation	Households Not Currently in the Sandwich Generation
My supervisor listens to our problems	68% agree	61% agree
I have been able to balance home and work life without hindering my career progression	72% agree	65% agree
This company provides family-friendly benefits to employees	59% agree	52% agree
Managers recognize the importance of your personal and family life	59% agree	60% agree
My manager pays attention to how people feel at work	64% agree	53% agree
This company is sensitive to the needs of employees	50% agree	50% agree

employees on a regular basis may likely be aware of the impending special need or circumstance, and thus are better prepared to respond.

In instances in which the request for special accommodation or intervention comes out of the blue, managers may have to work with the employee, the rest of the work team and other departments to meet the request. Managers can prepare for these eventualities by working with their counterparts to develop contingency plans and approaches. In some cases, managers themselves may initiate an intervention for an employee facing special needs or circumstances. Managers who are aware of their employees' stress, burnout or frustrations may proactively work with the employee to adjust workflow or schedules, adjust work processes, alleviate interactions with stakeholders or facilitate similar arrangements.

Organizationally initiated identification of employees with special needs or circumstances happens, too. In this instance, senior leaders or HR may be privy to a matter affecting the employee's ability to perform his/her job effectively, and may proactively work with the employee or manager to alleviate job-related stressors or distractions. Issues such as pending legal cases or an internal investigation affecting the employee, the inability to be medically released to resume work (even if an employee feels otherwise ready) and restrictions of employee access to certain aspects of work — for medical, personal, proprietary or other reasons — may compel organizationally initiated identification and intervention related to employees with special needs or circumstances.

One important managerial variable, of course, is the extent to which employee situations are likely to be temporary or permanent. With physical disabilities, for example, an ongoing, reasonable accommodation may be needed, whereas in adjusting an employee's work schedule to permit the employee to take a required college class in the middle of the workday may have a much shorter time horizon.

Operate With Fairness and Discretion When Handling Sensitive Employee Matters

The admittedly personal nature of accommodations and interventions related to employees with special needs or circumstances requires a degree of fairness, discernment and discretion on the part of managers. Fairness implies that managers use their judgment to make decisions that are in the best interests of the organization, while weighing that against the unique and situational aspects of each special need or circumstance facing an employee. Different people have different issues that require different approaches from managers and organizations. While desirous to exercise consistency in making these types of decisions, the reality is that no two employees or special needs or circumstances will be the same. Thus, managers must become comfortable making fair decisions that balance personal, professional and organizational obligations in often competing yet coexisting ways.

Necessarily related to fairness, of course, is the ability for managers to exercise discretion in handling sensitive employee matters. Issues related to health, wellness and personal challenges should be treated as confidential, and information should only be shared with others in the organization — including an employee's co-workers — after obtaining express permission from the affected employee. Managers are encouraged to consult with their HR professionals and, in some cases, legal counsel, for guidance on how to handle certain high-stakes special needs and circumstances. Generally, however, managers should be able to make decisions that serve the organization well, while treating individual employees with the dignity and respect they deserve.

Provide Flexible Work Arrangements, as Feasible

To meet the needs of both individuals and organizations, managers can provide flexibility in areas such as scheduling and the nature of work. From a scheduling standpoint, there are several options to help employees meet personal and professional obligations. First, flex time is an approach that permits variable start and finish times for employees, usually with a requirement of a minimum number of core hours worked per day, and a minimum number of required hours per week. For example, employees might have the option of arriving between 6 a.m. and 9 a.m. and departing between 3 p.m. and 6 p.m.; the core hours of work are between 9 a.m. and 3 p.m.

Closely related to flex time is the compressed workweek, in which workers can work four 10-hour days, three 12-hour days or another compressed schedule. Annualized hours allow for employees to accumulate a minimum number of total hours per year, largely on their own schedule. Providing part-time employment, permitting telecommuting or arranging for employees to share jobs are all strategies managers can employ — either temporarily or on a longer-term basis — for employees needing flexibility to handle a special need or circumstance in their lives.

Develop Specific Interventions to Address Employee Needs

Depending on the employee population served by the organization, a number of interventions can be developed. Child-care assistance permits employees with young children to find affordable, quality care for children, and this often is subsidized (in full or in part) by the organization. Elder-care assistance provides many of the same benefits and services as child-care assistance, only with an emphasis on the unique caregiving and other needs of an employee's elderly parent or relative. As noted, some employees find themselves as part of the Sandwich Generation, caught in the midst of providing child and elder care simultaneously.

Another approach is offering employees the ability to buy, sell, bank or donate time off. This permits individuals to customize their time-off arrangements, within guidelines and limitations, and, in some cases, it allows workers to sell or give away time off to other employees who need or value this benefit. To be fair, the interventions described often are ones that serve the macro-organizational environment, yet it is the employee's direct manager that often facilitates awareness about, and encouragement and/or approval for use of, these interventions.

Assess, Clarify and Prioritize Approaches to Engage Employees With Special Needs or Circumstances

Managers should work with each other, their employees, HR and senior leaders to assess, clarify and prioritize approaches to engage employees with special needs and circumstances. Inventorying current approaches, sharing best practices within the organization, surveying employees and benchmarking with other organizations all are actions managers can initiate and support in this endeavor. To be sure, while many approaches aimed at employees with special needs and circumstances are worthwhile, it is impractical and unnecessary to initiate and implement all such approaches. Thus, it is necessary to analyze, clarify and prioritize those approaches that are likely to have the greatest utility, appeal and impact on individual employees and the organization. Outlining approaches and interventions based on time and cost matrix is helpful (time: immediate, short-term and long-term interventions; cost: no-cost, low-cost and moderate- to high-cost interventions). Creating an environment that signals to employees that the organization is concerned with their overall well-being helps the firm find, motivate and keep its increasingly diverse workforce, while also meeting both individual and organizational needs.

Action Planning Log for Engaging *Employees with Special Needs or Circumstances*

Employee Name	Specific Actions Planned to Engage Employee

What is the organization doing especially well to engage *Employees with Special Needs or Circumstances*?

In what ways can the organization improve its efforts to engage *Employees with Special Needs or Circumstances*?

chapter 12
ENHANCING MANAGERIAL
EFFECTIVENESS THROUGH
WORKFORCE ENGAGEMENT

How Can Managers and Supervisors Enhance Effectiveness Through Workforce Engagement?

Making Work More Engaging
- For the employee
- Through job responsibilities
- In the work environment

Making Work More Engaging for the Employee

Managers can make work more satisfying for the employee by emphasizing identity, significance and opportunities to improve skills and interests during the performance of the job. Identity involves letting individual employees know what their specific job responsibilities entail, what outcomes their work is expected to produce and how their work is related to other jobs. Significance permits individual employees to realize why the work they undertake is important, how their job affects the larger scheme of the organization and the consequences (positive or negative) their work has on a product, service, customer, business process or solution. Finally, opportunities to improve skills and interests focus on providing employees with information about the present and future skills needed by the organization; ways to acquire, practice and improve additional skills; opportunities to broaden work experiences and contributions beyond one's immediate job; and the ability to integrate personal and professional interests, as appropriate.

Making Work More Engaging Through Job Responsibilities

Managers can make work more satisfying for employees by including variety, autonomy and pay for performance as part of job responsibilities. Variety requires that job responsibilities include an array of activities that draw upon and develop employee skills and interests; a rotation of tasks to avoid monotony; depth of assignments to increase understanding, proficiency and expertise; and breadth of assignments to increase cross-training capabilities and flexibility. Autonomy requires that job responsibilities provide appropriate discretion in managing workflow;

decision-making authority consistent with the scope of work performance expected; individual access to tools and resources necessary to perform the job; and sufficient discretion to determine communications across departmental and/or organizational lines. Finally, pay for performance requires that job responsibilities should reward high-quality work outcomes; meritorious contributions from individual efforts; and the acquisition and use of value-added knowledge and skills.

Making Work More Engaging in the Work Environment

Managers can make work more satisfying for employees by ensuring fairness and equity, feedback, pleasant physical workspaces and positive relationships in the work environment. *Fairness* treats unequal people differently (for example, individuals performing the same job and producing different levels of output or quality). *Equity*, however, treats different people the same (for example, providing equal opportunities to all qualified candidates and employees). *Feedback* provides employees with guidance on what constitutes excellent, satisfactory and poor performance; timely and accurate examples of how their work is viewed by peers, managers/supervisors and customers; and information on changes within the industry, the organization and their unit/department. *Pleasant physical workspaces* include safe and ergonomically correct work stations; well-maintained, updated and properly functioning equipment; and an aesthetically pleasing and enjoyable work experience. Finally, *positive working relationships* encourage open, cordial and candid communication between employees, managers and other stakeholders; constructive feedback on ways to improve work experiences; and respect for individual contributions and differences.

Outcomes of Engaging Work

- Financial outcomes
- Reputation outcomes
- Quality outcomes
- Relationship outcomes

Financial Outcomes

When an organization engages employees through satisfying work experiences, this typically translates into improved productivity, efficiency and retention. Additionally, employees who have a high personal attachment to the organization and are committed to their work generate enhanced relationships with customers. This typically yields greater revenue per employee, higher profitability and increased market share for customers. Finally, engaged employees behave in ways that exercise stewardship over the organization's resources. Abuse of policies, "shrinkage" and employee theft, and questionable medical, workers' compensation and other similar claims tend to decrease. Thus, the extent to which employees are engaged in performing meaningful work has a bottom-line impact.

Reputation Outcomes

Organizations that employ workers who actually enjoy their work often are viewed as excellent employers. This is evidenced by the fact that employees will have a high likelihood to recommend the organization as a good place to work and as a good place with which to conduct business. This leads to an enhanced ability for the organization to attract the type of talent it needs to be successful. In some instances, positive reputations have led to external recognition (e.g., a best company to work for list) of excellent employee-centric practices. Finally, employees who are engaged in their organizations tend to doubt negative information heard about the organization in the press or elsewhere, and are willing to support the organization in times of crises.

Quality Outcomes

Organizations that have workforces that care about how work is performed, products are produced and business processes are maximized will tend to have environments characterized by high quality and an emphasis on excellence. This is evidenced by measures such as error rates, product defects, product returns and customer complaints received. Additionally, a quality-minded culture unleashes creativity among workers, leading to an increased ability to design new products, services and processes, and to adopt and implement a continuous-improvement mind-set and culture.

Relationship Outcomes

When employees are engaged in satisfying work, the relationships they have with co-workers, supervisors, customers and business partners tend to be enhanced. In such environments, employees tend to be willing to work harder, go the extra mile to ensure customer satisfaction and perform work beyond the minimum level of acceptable performance. Enhanced relationships among and between stakeholders also can positively affect the other outcomes of meaningful work: financial, reputation and quality. There is a compelling business case for the creation of engaging, satisfying work experiences for employees. Some of the likely actions that might result from a workforce that is unengaged include, but are not limited to:

- Employee turnover
- Customer dissatisfaction
- Poor financial performance
- Lack of innovation
- Theft and unethical practices
- Conflict between management and labor
- Poor or diminished quality or service.

Thus, there is the need for organizations to continuously identify, implement, monitor, evaluate and improve specific practices that contribute to workforce engagement.

10 Principles of Engagement Every Manager and Supervisor Should Know

1. Realize that perception often overshadows reality.
2. Train employees so they can leave, or else they'll leave.
   a. Employees want the ability to "move up, over or out."
3. Train managers so they can lead, or else they'll leave.
   a. Competing "mountaintops" of consistency versus flexibility
   b. "Valley of ambiguity" causes issues.
4. Align espoused values with actual practice (do more than just talk the talk).
5. Manage performance every day of the year with intentional, explicit and continual feedback.
6. Practice the principle of "fire fast, hire slow."
7. Recognize that training is an investment, not a cost.
8. Identify performance problems and fix them quickly.
9. Hold managers accountable for employee-centric measures.
10. Remember that employees tend to quit a boss, not a company.

How Managers and Supervisors Can Assess Their Organization's Engagement Efforts

The reader is encouraged to use his/her own organization (or a unit therein) to assess current strengths to leverage opportunities for improvement — and to develop specific recommendations — as they relate to workforce engagement. Begin by identifying key informants (a mix of senior leaders, HR professionals, managers and individual-contributor employees) who are knowledgeable about the organization, its history and its workforce-related practices. Using the questions in Appendix A, ask key informants about all of the components of work-force engagement, drawn from the 10 types of employees outlined in this book.

After collecting the information, analyze the findings, identify common themes, and synthesize and summarize the results. Then, share this information with the key informants who initially provided the answers to the questions. Finally, involve colleagues who can assist to:

- Brainstorm possible recommendations for improvements.
- Develop specific strategies and timelines for implementation.
- Identify indicators of performance (e.g., reduced turnover, enhanced employee satisfaction, lower absenteeism).
- Assign action items or responsibilities to people or departments who will champion or implement the recommendations.

Appendix B provides planning worksheets for engagement initiatives that will be helpful with this process.

Good luck — and please visit www.employeeholdem.com to share with us your ongoing successes and challenges in making workforce engagement work!

appendix A
QUESTIONS FOR KEY INFORMANTS

In engaging *new employees*, how well do managers in the organization ...

... determine the job a new employee is to undertake?

... select the right person, for the right job, at the right time?

... provide a realistic job preview?

... set challenging, yet achievable, performance expectations?

... offer meaningful on-the-job training and encourage questions?

... allocate appropriate tools and technology for work?

In engaging *mid-career employees*, how well do managers in the organization ...

... enhance work through job enlargement, enrichment and rotation?

... provide movement upward, laterally and, in some cases, outside the organization?

... invest in more long-term, career-oriented training?

... recognize that company reputation becomes more important to employees?

... manage performance in a more holistic, developmentally focused manner?

... identify and use employees as mentors for new and underperforming employees?

... connect high-potential employees to superstar and/or long-term employees?

... discuss with employees their continued "fit" with the job, work team and organization?

In engaging *underperforming employees*, how well do managers in the organization ...

... identify the underperforming employee?

... determine if performance deficiency is knowledge-/skill-related or attitude-/motivation-related?

... resist the urge to simply transfer the employee to another department?

... develop coordinated, appropriate interventions along with expectations, metrics and timetables for success?

... document performance and follow a progressive-discipline framework?

... practice the adage "fire fast, hire slow"?

In engaging *superstar employees*, how well do managers in the organization ...

... recognize that these employees tend to make decisions faster and expect results accordingly?

... link pay and performance more explicitly?

... provide other intangible rewards and recognition?

... fast-track superstar employees for training, promotion and other opportunities?

... avoid letting an otherwise well-intentioned and good company policy stand in the way of engaging superstars?

... manage effectively the manager-employee roles and relationships?

In engaging *returning employees*, how well do managers in the organization ...

... identify reasons why employees initially left and their motives for returning?

... assess the organization's willingness and ability to accommodate returning employees?

... ensure that returning employees are informed of any changes to organizational strategy, policies and procedures?

... handle special concerns or considerations related to a returning employee?

... evaluate the long-term effectiveness of providing options and opportunities to returning employees?

In engaging *transferred or promoted employees*, how well do managers in the organization ...

... use similar selection criteria for internal transfers or promotions as external hires?

... determine the scope of new roles and define clear performance expectations?

... invest heavily in training and development for newly transferred and/or promoted employees?

... identify the potential challenge of placing a superstar employee in a managerial role?

... provide coaching and mentoring, especially for managerial roles?

... recognize that once an employee is transferred or promoted, there is a tendency for the employee to want to be transferred or promoted again?

In engaging *long-term employees*, how well do managers in the organization ...

... capture and share knowledge of long-term employees with others?

... ensure these employees have meaningful work that positively impacts their identity?

... emphasize broader career- and professional-development aspects of organizational affiliation?

... implement reward, recognition and development approaches that make sense?

... use long-term employees as coaches/mentors for new and mid-career employees?

In engaging *temporary employees*, how well do managers in the organization ...

... recognize the role that temporary employees play in meeting organizational needs?

... identify the scope of work, set appropriate boundaries and manage expectations accordingly?

... provide necessary training, tools and technology for work performance?

... effectively manage feedback and performance management processes?

... treat temporary employees with common courtesy, dignity and respect?

In engaging *distance-based employees*, how well do managers in the organization ...

... determine the scope, nature and impact of distance-based employees on the organization?

... identify changes to management styles and approaches that must occur?

... allocate necessary tools and technology to manage employees?

... develop communication strategies and provide specific opportunities to keep distance-based employees connected to the organization?

... evaluate the effectiveness of work arrangements and make ongoing enhancements and improvements?

In engaging *employees with special needs or circumstances*, how well do managers in the organization ...

- ... recognize that employees appreciate managers that are concerned about their holistic well-being?
- ... identify employees facing special needs or circumstances?
- ... operate with fairness and discretion when handling sensitive employee matters?
- ... provide flexible work arrangements, as feasible?
- ... develop specific interventions to address employee needs?
- ... assess, clarify and prioritize approaches to engage employees with special needs or circumstances?

appendix B
PLANNING WORKSHEETS FOR EMPLOYEE ENGAGEMENT INITIATIVES

Initiative: _____

People and/or departments that need to be consulted/involved in initiative

Person/Department to Consult/Involve	Reason(s) Why this Person/Department Needs to Be Consulted/Involved

Situational analysis (internal/external considerations likely affecting the initiative)

Issue	Description/Notes
Internal Strengths	
Internal Weaknesses	
External Opportunities	
External Threats	

Performance indicators (measures to determine if the initiative is achieving results)

1.	
2.	
3.	
4.	
5.	

Resources needed to implement the initiative

Type	Resources Needed
Physical	
Financial	
Human	
Technological	
Other	

Action Item(s), timeline and responsibility for the initiative

Action Item(s)	Timeline	Responsibility